The Outer Limits of Edgar Cayce's Power

The Outer Limits of Edgar Cayce's Power

✳

The Cases that Baffled the Legendary Psychic

Edgar Evans Cayce & Hugh Lynn Cayce

PARAVIEW
Special Editions

New York

The Outer Limits of Edgar Cayce's Power was originally published
by A.R.E. Press in 1971.

Cover design by smythtype

ISBN: 1-931044-68-6
Library of Congress Catalog Number: 2003113670

PREFACE

Edgar Cayce's accuracy as a psychic has been the subject of many books. Some authors have illustrated his astounding ability by documenting cases in which individuals obtained relief from physical suffering. The so-called "physical readings," which comprise about 60% of all Cayce's readings, are the main source from which their cases were taken. Other authors have selected particular sets of readings, for example those mentioning Atlantis, as the basis for their books. In every instance the accuracy of Cayce's statements was stressed. Recent discoveries in the medical, archaeological, and other fields were quoted to show that Cayce was truly on target, if not ahead of his time.

Was Cayce ever wrong? Did he ever give information that was vague, misleading or downright false? What caused this breakdown of his unusual ability? Can we learn anything from his failures?

In this book we examine the Cayce readings that seem to be incorrect. In spite of an estimated 85% accuracy record, about as good as that of most modern doctors, there are readings in the files that must be rated as failures. By examining these few readings we may gain an insight into Cayce's psychic talents. Perhaps what we learn may apply to other psychics as well.

It is interesting to note that Edgar Cayce's unsuccessful readings stem not so much from the physical or even the life readings, as from a miscellaneous collection of readings which include such diverse subjects as missing people, oil wells, and buried treasure.

In the chapter entitled "The Nature of Psychic Perception" we look at the probable sources of Edgar Cayce's information for clues as to why these particular readings were failures. Since what applies to Cayce in particular probably applies to other psychics in general, this study should help us better understand psychic phenomena.

If a baseball player with a .480 batting average strikes out in one game, he is not written off for the rest of the season. Although the majority of Edgar Cayce's readings were accurate, that does not mean they were all accurate. Nor does it follow that because a few were incorrect that they were all incorrect. Two cases that were recently checked, more than fifty years after they were given, may illustrate the point.

In 1925 and again in 1931 Edgar Cayce stated that long ago the Nile River once flowed into the Atlantic Ocean. Back in 1925 and even later in 1931 there was no way to check these pronouncements. It was not until 1986 that radar pictures taken from the space shuttle showed that the old course of the Nile indeed flowed west into the Atlantic instead of maintaining its present direction north into the Mediterranean Sea.

In 1984 charcoal fragments taken from mortar between the blocks of the Great Pyramid of Giza were carbon dated. This was to check statements in several Cayce readings that the Great Pyramid was built about 10,500 B.C. Although the dates from seventeen samples proved to be approximately 400 years older than accepted Egyptian chronology—about 2500 B.C.—none dated back as far as Cayce's claim.

Why was Cayce right in one instance and wrong in the other? We don't know. But each case must be judged on its own merits. We should strive to learn from our failures as well as from our successes. We hope you will read this book with that thought in mind.

Contents

CHAPTER 1

Successes and Failures

Now you will have before you the body of Vera Smith, who is at 2405 West 7th Street, Dayton, Ohio. You will go over this body carefully, examine it thoroughly, and tell me the conditions you find at the present time; giving the cause of the existing conditions, also the suggestions for the help and relief for this body. You will speak distinctly at a normal rate of speech. You will answer the questions that may be asked.

Gertrude Cayce read this suggestion over again for the fifth time. Her husband lay on the studio couch to her left, his hands crossed over his stomach; a brightly colored afghan that she had crocheted for him was pulled up to his interlaced fingers. His eyes were closed, he breathed regularly and evenly. There was no response from the sleeping man. At a nearby desk, the secretary, Gladys Davis, waited. A calendar on the desk showed the date as Thursday, February 12, 1934.

Edgar Cayce—known today to hundreds of thousands of people as the "Sleeping Prophet," to hundreds of people as a good Sunday school teacher, and to us as Dad—slept for an hour and a half that day without speaking. This was one of perhaps twelve times over a period of forty-three years when he did not respond to the suggestion that was given to him twice a day on an average of eight times each week.

Hundreds of miles away, in Dayton, Ohio, Vera Smith waited, not knowing exactly what to expect. When she had written to Edgar Cayce in Virginia Beach, Virginia, at the suggestion of a friend who had known about the Cayces when they lived in Dayton, she had been told to state exactly where she would be at 3 P.M. on the afternoon of February 12th. Nothing was asked about her illness. She volunteered no information. In her first letter, she had said, "I've been sick for some time. The doctors seem to disagree on what is wrong. Will you please give me a reading?" Within a few days she would receive not a reading, but a short note from Edgar Cayce saying that he had been unable to get the reading. Another date would be given, and again Miss Smith would be asked to say where she would be, this time at 10 A.M. on February 25.

What happened? Why didn't Edgar Cayce follow his regular procedure and talk about this woman? Was something wrong with him, with his wife who gave him the suggestion, with Vera Smith in Dayton, Ohio? Just how accurate were the Edgar Cayce psychic readings? Did he ever make mistakes? If so, was there any explanation for them? What kind of information was likely to be right; what likely to be wrong? These are some of the questions this book will attempt to answer.

Because there are more than 50,000 typewritten pages of stenographic transcripts of Edgar Cayce's readings on file in the national headquarters of the Association, and because there are now over 200,000 index cards with subject headings, it is possible to examine what Cayce said on almost any subject.

The Association for Research and Enlightenment in Virginia Beach, Virginia, a psychical research society, preserved and today is continuing to check, compare, and experiment with the data in these readings. In this volume, we will discuss both his successes and failures, touching partly on incidents and types of readings where he seemed to have been wrong. In some ways, his failures tell us more about Edgar Cayce and his psychic "reach" than an examination of those cases where he was accurate.

Hopefully, this book will establish a basis for further psychic research. Whoever comes to Virginia Beach to read the details of the lost mines or buried treasure or to probe the files for readings on odd subjects will find thousands of physical and life readings that have proven helpful, for this organization is devoted to studying them for possible future benefit. Here there is one of the best libraries in the United States on psychic subjects and a bookroom filled with the latest works on associated phenomena. In the activities of the A.R.E. one may discover a new outlook on life. True treasure will not be found in the sand hills of Virginia, the deserts of Arizona, or in the mountains of Arkansas, but within one's own self. The search for understanding one's self and one's relation to God and one's fellow man will lead to the greatest treasure of all. This was the major focus of the vast majority of the Edgar Cayce readings.

CHAPTER 2

Edgar Cayce As We Knew Him *

As the elder of two sons, the early days in Selma, Alabama, bring back memories like the following:

The paper felt slick as I rubbed it gently just as my father explained I should. The tray of "developer," as Dad called it, smelled like the chemistry lab at school. The red light glowed dimly but my eyes had adapted to the darkness. A face, then another one, appeared on the print under my fingers. There was a boy and a girl and a bicycle. "That's it," Dad said, "take it out now and drop it into the fixing bath; then later it has to be moved into the washing tray." I was learning how to develop Kodak pictures. My father, Edgar Cayce, was a photographer and about the best one in the state, I guessed, maybe in the whole world. I knew he was about to open a new office in Marion, Alabama, because the girls' school there had given him the job of making pictures for the annual. "We'll make some money off of this one, Muddie," he had said to my mother, Gertrude. It was only last week that the State Police had come, asking Dad to find a picture of a man who had stolen a lot of money from a bank. Dad had the picture, too.

It was exciting living in the studio apartment. My friends pestered me to let them see the room where Dad took pictures. It was a large

*Written by Hugh Lynn Cayce.

room on the third floor. Overhead was a ceiling of glass—a skylight, Dad called it. There were shades on rolls so you could have just the amount of light you needed. Canvas screens with scenes painted on both sides moved on rollers and could be used to make rooms when we played "detective" and "cops and robbers." All kinds of furniture was sitting around to be used as part of the pictures Dad took. No one minded when Dad shooed us out. We generally ended up in the kitchen to examine my mother's well-filled cookie jar.

Many times I had overheard ladies talking about their children. "Mr. Cayce, I don't know how you do it. Howard never takes a good picture with any other photographer, but he always smiles for you." Dad had taken so many children's pictures that he had plenty to put up on the edge of a big circle in his showcase on the street. The hands of a clock moved around the circle. When they stopped, the parents of the child closest to each hand got a big picture tinted by my mother.

As I let my mind go back over the days in Selma, it is easy to remember a quite different kind of Edgar Cayce than the one now known to thousands of people as the "Sleeping Prophet." How do you describe a man who has almost become a legend? How can you describe a man who was so normal and natural in many ways, and yet was possessed of a strange power that was to affect the lives of thousands of people who never saw him?

My brother, Edgar Evans, and I remember him as someone who loved to play games with us. With me it was checkers, parcheesi, and rook. In later years, it was dominoes and caroms. And with both of us, though we are eleven years apart in age, he fished, golfed, and bowled. He was not good at golf, but he loved it and he could take either of us at bowling. One Christmas we got a croquet set and discovered that our father was a one-handed expert.

Both my brother and I went to Sunday school and church and grew to love it, because Edgar Cayce made Sunday school classes an exciting experience and Bible reading something to look forward to.

Back in Selma, where I grew up through grade school and early high school, Dad enabled me to supplement my allowance of 25¢ a week by learning how to frame pictures. He could make anything with a saw, nails, and a hammer.

It wasn't all work by any means. There were Sunday school picnics and Christian Endeavor activities on Sunday afternoon and nights. Sometimes we went to state conventions and Dad became a state officer in the Junior Christian Endeavor Program. Our church, the First Christian Church, was very proud of the youth activity he engendered. There were group pictures in the paper when awards were presented to him at the conventions.

I have often told my brother of the war on rats that Dad and I carried on. When he was little, I told him we "protected" him from the rats. Dad's studio combined with our family apartment was over a wholesale drug company that was next to a wholesale grocery store. The rats grew fat in the grocery store and cut through into our building. When the cats installed by the grocery company began to chase them, Dad and I trapped them and sometimes actually fought the big ones when they were cornered in our rooms. To an eight-year-old, they were as big as wild boars and just as fierce.

One of the things both my brother and I remember (he from his grade- and high-school years in Virginia Beach and I from my school years in Selma) was Dad's love of making jellies, preserves, brandied peaches, and wine. During Prohibition, Dad was investigated not as a psychic but as a possible moonshiner because he bought such large quantities of sugar. He gladly stood over the pots in our kitchen, both in Selma and Virgina Beach, carefully cooking the jelly mixtures. He was proud of the fact that his jelly never included preservatives of any kind. He cooked it to just the right point to make it gel. As a wine-maker, Dad experimented. The best wine he ever made was from the grapes that grew wild on the sandhills of Virginia Beach. The whole family would have small glasses of wine whenever Dad "bottled" from the big stone jars in the basement.

As we grew up, both my brother and I were encouraged to bring our friends to the house. Mother always had something ready to eat, and Dad was friendly and easy with people of any age. When my brother was old enough for scouting, Dad urged me to help with a local scout troop in Virginia Beach. It was in connection with the activity of this scout troop that we discovered another facet of our father's wide range of accomplishments.

Our scout troop got permission to build a cabin on a then undeveloped wooded area on Linkhorn Bay in Virginia Beach. We had raised money by newspaper salvage, bake sales, work at odd jobs, and scout fairs. Businessmen and families helped, and we bought lumber and bricks and moved them, literally board by board and brick by brick, to the proposed site. One scout father could drill water wells and he tried to find some good water for us so we could build the cabin over the well. Twice he hit only brackish water, which is easy to find in Virginia Beach.

I mentioned our problem to Dad. He insisted that we go right over to the site, and proposed to find the water for us. I drove him out to the intended cabin area. On the way he asked me to stop near a peach tree on the roadside. He cut a Y-shaped branch and continued to trim it during the rest of the ride.

When we arrived at the edge of the woods, he walked with me for a mile to an area near the bay that we had selected for the cabin. He held the peach tree switch in his hands with the fingers turned in and the little branches of the Y slightly bent. The single, small branch stuck out in front of his chest as he began to walk back and forth over the ground. Now and then it dipped down. He would back up and walk forward again. Finally the branch began to turn down and, as I watched, the bark twisted off the two small branches that he held tightly. Finally, he marked a place and drove a stick there. Then he stood at this point with the single branch sort of bobbing up and down. He counted to himself and then told me that we would get good water at 32 feet. We drove the well there and got plenty of fresh water at 32½ feet. Apparently Edgar Cayce was also a dowser.

In Selma, Alabama, there was little opportunity for Dad to express his love for growing things. However, in my brother's growing-up period in Virginia Beach, he became involved in many gardening and chicken-raising projects. Good chickens were raised from hatched eggs and, strangely, a new war was started with rats who ate the feed and attacked the small chickens. My father encouraged Edgar Evans to keep the rats at bay with a .22 rifle. He used to shoot the rats from the backyard steps. He and Dad trapped them, too.

Gardening was our father's constant part-time activity, and he frequently had the earliest peas, the biggest strawberries, and the largest beds of asparagus in town. Both Edgar Evans and I were drafted now and then to work in the garden, but we never worked alone. Dad was right there telling stories of his childhood or asking us questions to keep our minds off the working time. He always worked harder than we did and stayed longer, digging around each plant, touching them, and talking with them. Growing things was very important to him. It could safely be said that he had a green thumb, a very green thumb.

Dad enjoyed ordering plants and trees from catalogues. At one time in Virginia Beach he had as many as fifteen or sixteen different fruit and flowering trees, especially some rather unusual ones, like quince, crabapple and formosa, that were growing in a small backyard.

Our father spent some time almost every day during good weather fishing for small perch in the little lake back of the house in Virginia Beach. He built a pier out into the water and put a comfortable seat on the end of it. The sun was hot during the summer, so he planted a small willow tree in a tar-lined box filled with soil and attached a rope to it so that he could pull the floating tree out to the end of the pier to shade him. Dad loved to fish. We have pictures of him with sailfish in Florida, salmon in Maine, a string of trout from the St. Lawrence, and spot from Chesapeake Bay. On one occasion, I was with him in Texas when he outfished everyone in the party and then cleaned twice as many as the other men as they prepared a Texas fish-fry.

Dad didn't confine his use of the hammer and saw to small objects.

At one house he involved us in the building of a whole new room, and at another, we built a garage.

My brother and I were encouraged to have pets. Our dogs—a whole series of them—were just dogs. All of them were fond of our father. There were also rabbits, canaries, goldfish, and a parrot. The latter has been made famous by Tom Sugrue's stories about him in *There is a River,* the first biography of Edgar Cayce. This parrot loved to sit on my father's shoulder and gently touch his ear. We all watched this in awe for we had seen the same parrot break a lead pencil easily in his sharp beak. I say "his" almost by habit. It was only during the parrot's last days with us that he layed an egg, built a nest out of newspapers, and became "Miss Polly."

In trying to remember those first years in Virginia Beach, it's hard to realize how strange it seemed to move to a deserted little summer resort in September 1925, when everything was closed. The readings had insisted that this was the place where the "work" would grow. My brother was seven when we arrived; I was eighteen. No one knew us. Few people knew where we had gone when we left Dayton, Ohio. For amusement, my mother, Dad, Miss Gladys the secretary, and I (and at times my brother) held "information nights" and reported on news events and obscure facts of general interest. My mother always turned up with the most unusual information. There were evenings for games, also. Dominoes, caroms, crockinole, and parcheesi helped pass many lonely evenings.

Edgar Cayce didn't read anything but the newspaper and the Bible. The few books in our library were gift copies of novels and books of poetry that Dad had given my mother during his early bookstore days.

Dad was a great storyteller. He didn't tell jokes very much, but his stories were frequently humorous. Both my brother and I loved the stories of his dog, who grew up with him on the farm outside of Hopkinsville, Kentucky. This was a very fierce dog, according to him, who once killed other dogs when they attacked a herd of sheep, and on one occasion he killed a man who tried to attack my father's aunt.

Sometimes you can tell a great deal about a man from his letters. The following extracts are taken from letters to me and my brother, first when we were in college and then while we were in the army. These letters kept us posted not only on the work Dad was doing, but also on his hobbies, gardening, fishing and caring for the animals.

When we first moved to Virginia Beach, only the road from Norfolk and Atlantic Avenue, parallel with the ocean, were paved. Dad recorded the first paving of the side streets in a letter to me dated December 6, 1926, when I was a freshman in college:

I understand from hearsay and from some remarks in the local paper that the City of Virginia Beach is preparing to pave all side streets from 11th to 40th street. . . . I presume we will be included. . . . It will certainly make a great difference in the appearance of the "berg."

Everywhere we moved, Dad became involved in teaching Sunday school.

Well, I started off teaching Sunday school class yesterday morning! Mr. Ramsey of the Presbyterian Church, you know, has asked me several times to take a class up there (April 4, 1927).

On the flowers and garden he wrote on September 23, 1927, and again on February 28, 1928:

Well, I got my rose garden all prepared and have written the rose growers to know whether it's done right or not. I'm anxious to see them in the ground and growing. I guess I'll be watching them every day when I do put them in.

The garden is in pretty good shape. Watermelon and canteloupe hills made —shrubbery here to put out but didn't have all my ground in shape so had to put if off a few days. Fix it though when the ground is right—hope will have a nice looking place this summer!

During the last year of his life, Dad grew sentimental as he grew tired, but now and then some incident stirred him up. He described one such incident in his letter to me of May 24, 1944:

You know I was very much put out the other day when a man phoned me and wanted to know if I wanted you home. Possibly he is in a position to do something about it. But when he made this provision, possibly you can imagine, knowing me as well as you do, what happened: "I want a reading *today* on my wife." As usual I blew up and it wasn't good for my blood pressure these days.

Even as far back as 1942 Dad began to feel the pressure. *There is a River,* the Sugrue biography, had been published and magazine articles had begun to bring quantities of mail. He wrote to Ecken, as he called my brother, on February 13, 1942:

Have such a bad cold . . . was abed day before yesterday, got up but this morning feel like going back to bed again if didn't have a meeting tonight would. But feel as if my race is about run, have done nothing to brag or boast of, haven't done so very many things am ashamed of, have tried to set for you and Bubber a fair example, advise you as best as have known how, tried to give each of you a fair education, and to assist you to live in this world, that suddenly seems gone mad, but is really an outgrowth of man's seeking the gratification of selfish desires rather than the will of God. Christian love and Christian grace is after all an individual thing, and is very true, so long as to our own selves we are true we will not be false to any, but that is not from the material angle of life at all, from the spiritual. Does the individual so live that he as a man is working with God among his fellow men there is a place for that man. For the earth and the fullness thereof is the Lord's. And His will, His purpose with man will not be placated. Many wish to hurry—and oft man has to do that to meet the evil as is abroad, but deep down inside there is the PEACE as if of His making and is his promise to man—"MY PEACE I GIVE YOU NOT AS THE WORLD KNOWS PEACE BUT PEACE AS COMES FROM GOD." And that Peace may be the pleasure of every man who keeps his heart, his purpose right with God. So my message to you during these trying hours is to live as not to be ashamed ever to meet thy maker. There will be much to be done when this war is over. More of those who have His purpose in mind will be saved than others—or there is a purging, that we as individuals and as a nation may bear better fruit in the work of the Lord.

CHAPTER 3

What Edgar Cayce Did

The Edgar Cayce readings date from 1901, when we know that he gave the first information on himself from an unconscious state. A variety of stenographers, including court reporters, were brought in to record the first readings. Unfortunately, copies of those early readings were not preserved. At the present time, there are a total of 14,246 individual copies of different readings in the files of the Association. They average three and a half single-spaced typewritten pages. The earliest dated reading on file was given in 1909. There are 523 readings dating between 1909 and 1923. From 1923 through January 1945, when Edgar Cayce died in Virginia Beach, every psychic reading that he gave was stenographically recorded. The following is a breakdown of the various types of readings.

There are 8,976 physical readings. These include both the first readings and what came to be called check physical readings, which were sometimes as long as the original reading. Several check readings could be given sequentially. These were especially helpful during the days when the hospital was in operation and one patient's name after another could be presented. Edgar Cayce would make comments and bring each case up to date. It was found from questioning in the individual physical readings that, generally speaking, Edgar Cayce's information was more helpful when given on a specific type of ailment rather than from the basis of questions of a general nature. However, there were a few readings given on general subjects. These usually were taken when individual doctors were interested in asking questions. There were two readings given on leukemia, one general reading on cancer, one on multiple sclerosis, one on polio and one on the common cold.

The second largest category dealt with what we have called life readings and check life readings. These life readings had to do specifically with psychological rather than physical problems which were facing people. There were questions about vocational guidance, marriage problems and human relation difficulties of various kinds. For example, from this group, there were 156 life readings for young people under the age of 15. In all, the total number was about 2,500 life readings, counting both first readings and second readings, which, in this case, were frequently as long or longer than the first life reading itself.

The first life readings were secured by presenting the sleeping Edgar Cayce with the following suggestion:

"You will have before you the body of——— (giving name and place of the individual at birth, the name at birth as given), and you will give the relation of this entity and the universe, and the universal forces, giving the conditions that are as personalities latent, and exhibited, in the present life. Also the former appearances in the earth's plane, giving time, place, name and that in that life which built or retarded the development for the entity, giving the abilities of the present entity and that to which it may attain, and how."

References were first made to what our father called mental planes of consciousness between incarnations in the earth. Symbols of the planets of our solar system were used, Mars, Venus, etc. These were spoken of not as places so much as states of awareness. Urges from these "experiences" were noted. Then from one to nine incarnations were described in brief paragraphs. Names, dates, and places were given along with urges, talents, and weaknesses from these lives focused on the present experience.

The check life readings were generally focused on one incarnation in the earth. Brief outlines of the life along with more details of the urges from this life affecting the present were given. Frequently a number of questions on specific problems being faced by the individual were answered.

The third largest category was 799 business readings, devoted exclusively to questions about business projects. The majority of these were secured by a few close friends of Edgar Cayce. Of a general nature under the business readings, there were 3 given on automatic vending machines. They are extremely interesting in the light of the unusual development of vending machines since that time. There were also 10 readings given on static eliminators, the forerunners of FM circuits, and 7 readings given on a motor suggesting a perpetual motion machine. There were also 12 readings given on two scenarios, neither of which was ever produced.

The fourth largest category, 667 readings, deals with dream interpretations. Here we count the actual number of readings that were devoted exclusively to the interpretation of dreams. In many individual readings there were additional questions involving interpretation of dream material.

The fifth largest category was 401 readings dealing with mental and spiritual questions. These were frequently concerned with what Edgar Cayce called "The purpose of the soul's entrance into the earth." As it turned out, the purposes that he described for the soul's entrance into the earth were frequently not quite in alignment with the conscious purposes that motivated the individual after his entrance here.

.From 1920 to 1923, Edgar Cayce became interested in securing money to further the building of a hospital through giving readings on oil wells. Sometimes readings dealt with mineral products rather than oil. In all, there were 223 readings on land. There were also 76 readings given on locating buried treasure.

There were 130 readings given for the first small group that undertook to study and apply discourses given by Edgar Cayce on spiritual laws. *The Search for God,* in two volumes, was compiled by this group based on these readings. More than 80,000 copies of these volumes have been sold. There were 65 readings given for a group that studied prayer and meditation for healing. Many of these readings were by questions following short discourses on the subject of healing. There were 9 readings of questions and answers given for various early Study Groups.

There were 116 readings that we call work readings. They were readings frequently requested by Edgar Cayce himself or by those who were directly involved in developing the activities of the Association, which was preserving and studying his readings. They were, for the most part, by questions and dealt with the ideals and purposes for expanding the Association program and with more mundane questions regarding membership, specific policies, and even detailed comments on such topics as the purchase of land and the development of a publication program. These work readings have been duplicated and are the basis for continuous study. Many of the present operations of the Association stem from these readings.

Thirty-five readings were given on aura charts. This information grew out of Edgar Cayce's reference in life readings to Life Seals and his meeting in 1941 with Nancy Lansdale, a charming lady who believed she saw colored geometric patterns near all living things. She drew and painted the geometric design she saw around Edgar Cayce. He asked about these images, and the comments in this first reading led to thirty-four others for different people. In their readings, unlike the Lansdale charts, he described a panel of scenes dealing with past lives with astrological signs on the borders.

There is an interesting group of readings on historical subjects, including 6 on prehistoric Egypt, 16 on the figure of Jesus, and 1 on the Mayan civilization. Thirteen readings were devoted to the general history of Atlantis. The subject of Atlantis had come up in various individual life readings where Edgar Cayce gave individual incarnations in prehistoric times, sometimes as frequently as he gave them in known historical periods.

Next, we come to a group of interesting readings by subject. We frequently wish we had had more of these. There were 24 readings on home and marriage, 3 on the general subject of reincarnation, 28 on world affairs. There were 14 readings on spiritualism, 1 on sunspots, 3 on sleep, 2 on the solar system, 1 on numerology, 6 on the general subject of psychic sources. Twelve readings were given on missing persons, 3 readings were given on child training, and 6 on gynecology.

Four readings were given on questions and answers on a book of extracts from the readings under the title *Psychic Phenomenon Through the Subliminal*. It was never submitted to a publisher.

Until the final readings are completely indexed and careful counts are made, there will be some shifting around in these figures, for it is sometimes almost a matter of opinion as to whether a reading is exclusively on one subject or another. Furthermore, the questions may be scattered and somewhat divided. At the present time, the indexing of the readings is about 98% complete.

CHAPTER 4

Was Edgar Cayce's Story a Hoax?

Is the whole Edgar Cayce story a mammoth hoax? This question must arise from time to time in the mind of a total skeptic. Admitting that he lay down and appeared to lose consciousness twice a day for years, how does one know that he wasn't conscious and just made all of the readings up? Before giving serious consideration to such an idea, the recorded data should be examined. Anyone who checks some of the details of the stories will soon realize that too many people (over 5,000) were involved in very personal ways for too long a period of time (43 years) for a blanket charge of fraud to apply.

Edgar Cayce gave his first psychic reading in 1901 and the last one in 1944. Stenographic copies of more than 14,000 of these readings exist today in typewritten form, transcribed by many different stenographers. Hundreds of persons still living heard and watched Edgar Cayce give these readings. Forty-three years of continuous conscious fabrication would be almost more amazing than considering the information as coming from the unconscious mind involving psychic perception. Let us explain.

Edgar Cayce said that he did not remember a single word he uttered in all the unconscious periods. Through the years, working as he did with doctors, lawyers, shrewd businessmen, psychologists, psychic investigators, members of his family, and hundreds of persons from all walks of life, he would have to have carefully masked his conscious language so as not to reveal his information that appeared in the reading. We must remember that many of those persons who did come to witness readings were looking for mistakes.

The conscious Edgar Cayce we knew could not possibly have continued such fabrication for 43 years. He was far too relaxed, far too involved in everyday affairs going on around him, far too unconcerned with what people thought about what he said in "the readings state" to have been alert to consciously manufacture the more than ten million words of which the readings were composed.

What about the possibility that Edgar Cayce's unconscious fabricated, pieced together bits of information contained in the suggestions, the letters, the questions? Many of the readings could be explained in this fashion, provided it could be established just how much was in the letters and questions Edgar Cayce read. There was a small group of close friends about whom Edgar Cayce came to know a great deal from personal letters and conversations. The fact that he did not just give readings for a closely knit group, but worked by mail for thousands of people he consciously never saw, makes it possible to survey the existing readings and correspondence for this information. While obviously, we cannot report on more than 14,000 documents, here is a summary of a random selection of 150 readings. Our random selection was made in the following manner.

There are 370 loose-leaf books of copies of Edgar Cayce readings in the A.R.E. Library, and each book contains from 15 to 20 readings. We decided to examine one reading from each of 150 different books. Slips of paper numbered from 1 to 20 were put into an envelope. After each book was taken from the shelf, a slip was drawn and the first reading of that number from the front of the book was tabulated.

By years the selected readings fall into the following arrangement:

1910–1 (reading)	1925–5
1921–1	1927–5

1922–6	1928–1
1923–6	1929–11
1924–6	1930–10
1931–6	1939–6
1932–5	1940–19
1933–3	1941–2
1934–5	1942–5
1935–8	1943–10
1936–4	1944–11
1937–4	
1938–10	

Of the group of 150 readings, 70 were women, 61 were men, and 19 were young persons from seven months to seventeen years of age. Forty-six people were present for their readings. Eighty-one averaged a distance of five hundred miles or less and five were three thousand miles or more from Edgar Cayce at the time the reading was given. In two instances, we do not have a record of where the people were.

In the random group, there were 110 physical readings, 34 life readings, 4 business readings, 1 dream reading, and 1 aura chart.

There were no reports from 74 people. There were 11 negative and 65 favorable reports.

Of the people who were not present for the reading, 42 gave some information about themselves. Of this number, 36 received additional information that, in our opinion, could not have been known to Edgar Cayce. Such information as the following was included in these statements: specific spinal lesions were noted by name, such as ninth dorsal, second lumbar; cramps in particular parts of the body; venereal disease; specific childhood accidents; recent operations; location of a tumor; right limb shorter than left; exact location of scar tissue; descriptions of specific skin infection; and so on.

Of the 150 persons, 35 gave no information about themselves. Their diagnoses included such items as the following: throat and larynx affected; constant tired feeling; high fever; adhesions in intestines formed; particularly bad diet; specific items to leave off mentioned; menstrual problems described; strep infection in intestinal tract; overactive heart reaction; references to poor handling of case; displaced pelvic organ; injury in shoulder area in past times; the second dorsal involved; kidneys in bad condition; eyestrain ten years before reading; temperature at times; childhood accidents, eardrum affected; detailed description of ear, eye, nose, and throat involvement and a specific digestive problem; person described as one of the directors of the town (local council as it was later reported); effects of a recent operation; pain in pit of stomach; and odors affecting the body.

As would be expected, it was from these two groups that the "good reports" of results in following the suggestions were received. If we project these figures on the basis of the random selection by multiplying by 100, thus relating them to the total number of readings now available for study (14,246), we come up with 3600 cases of additional information that apparently could not have been known to Edgar Cayce and 3500 persons on whom he gave information where no data was furnished to him.

Having observed Edgar Cayce over a period of many years as he met and talked with those who were present for reading, we are certain in our own minds that he obtained little information about the persons who came to him. In fact, he made a point of not talking to people prior to the readings. Frequently, the information included details unknown to the person involved or his family.

However, we must consider the facts now known from hypnotic regressions, as well as the more verifiable studies of Dr. Wilder Penfield, the famous Canadian neurosurgeon, on brain stimulation of forgotten childhood memories. These indicate that the unconscious perception of details is recorded far more accurately than we are consciously aware of. Such data would have been available to Edgar Cayce on people he saw and for whom he then gave information.

There were 11 negative reports in the sample of 150 readings. This projected figure comes to 1100 readings that were considered inadequate at the time.

This still leave 35 persons out of 150 who were not seen by Edgar Cayce and about whom he had no information of any kind. On our projection this figure rises to 3500 people. Compare this with the report of 65 our of 150 who reported favorable results, projecting this figure to 6500. It would seem that this data would be worthy of careful study.

Perhaps an even fairer picture can be given by applying the percentage figures from 150 random studies to the total number of people who had readings from Edgar Cayce—over five thousand different people.

Eleven persons out of 150 reported negatively. This is 7.3%, and, projected to 5,000 different people in 43 years, this would indicate 360 negative reports.

Sixty-five people out of 150 reported favorable results. This is 43.3% and, projected, would be 2,165 positive reports.

Now we should keep in mind that the reports show accuracy of results in following the information, not just accuracy of the diagnosis. During the times these readings were being given, 1901–1944, psychic studies were not only being criticized, they were scoffed and laughed at. We think that many more of Edgar Cayce's readings would have proven accurate and helpful had they been followed and had the patients reported on them.

To summarize the study of 150 readings selected at random:

No Reports	74 readings, or approximately	.... 50%
Negative Reports	11 readings, or approximately	.... 7%
Positive Reports	65 readings, or approximately	.... 43%
	150	100%

Note that "reports" refer to written reports. It is probable that many of the cases listed as "no reports" made a verbal report in person or by phone but left no written record.

Considering only the 76 readings in the survey for which there are written reports: 11 negative is 14.4%, and 65 positive is 85.5%.

Assuming that the ratio of positive to negative results remains the same in the cases not reported, and applying the random survey to the 14,246 readings on file, Cayce's accuracy of 85% compares favorably to that of modern physicians.

CHAPTER 5

Locating Missing Persons

One of the psychic gifts of the well-known Dutch sensitive, Gerard Croiset, seems to be the ability to locate missing persons, especially children. This focus on children stems from an early emotional involvement described in Jack Pollack's *Croiset—The Clairvoyant.*

Today many of Croiset the clairvoyant's images stem from his own childhood experiences. "Like many other paragnosts, he unconsciously searches for events in the lives of others that are associatively related to those in his own," states Dr. Tenhaeff. For example, Croiset has been extraordinarily successful in locating drowned children. His power in describing places and conditions have stunned the police and parents. This uncanny ability probably stems from Gerard himself having nearly drowned himself when he was eight years old. The event had a profound effect upon him.

A very small percentage of Edgar Cayce's readings (.08%) were devoted to missing persons, and the majority of these deal with two people. In all, there were 12 readings on this subject of which 8 were on two cases. While Edgar Cayce was apparently never kidnapped or lost himself, there were a few times when he did help locate a person when the request for help came from someone close to the individual for whom the information was sought. At such times, a direct telepathic-clairvoyant connection seemed to be established with the unconscious mind of the lost person. Missing person requests that came from distantly connected persons did not produce good results.

In one case described here—a man who ran away with the intention of committing suicide—the mind of the man himself may have blocked efforts to find him. Only after days of Cayce's efforts to subconsciously contact this man's mind was he successfully located.

The strange world of thought forms has been called by various names. To William James, the eminent American psychologist, it was "a stream of mind." Carl Jung, the well-known Swiss psychiatrist, who worked with and later broke with Sigmund Freud, called it "the collective unconscious." The great Catholic scholar, Pierre Teilhard de Chardin, called it "the universal mind." Hindu philosophy calls it "the Akashic record." Whatever its true nature may be, certainly the entanglements of interrelated thought patterns create barriers that are apparently confusing to the best of psychic talents. Edgar Cayce was no exception here. The following cases may offer real insight into the functioning of psychic perception in a thought-form world that we perceive "through a glass darkly." Let us begin with two simple cases.

On July 11, 1920, the following suggestion was given to Edgar Cayce, then a photographer in Selma, Alabama: "Information is desired as to the whereabouts of Miss #953, who was at Caswell, Baldwin County, Alabama, at Walker Cottage, Wednesday night, July 7th." Here is a definite time and person focus, in this case, requested by a brother. (Caswell was a rest home.)

Edgar Cayce answered:

We have had the body before. [It is known that Edgar Cayce had given physical readings for this person for which no copies now exist.] A message on the 8th to home was given someone else to post. It has been delayed. The message will reach home tomorrow early. She will be at home tomorrow. On way now. Delayed. She will be separated from someone before she reaches home. There has been sickness someone else, but she is all right.

The brother verbally reported that this proved to be correct. There is no record of a further reading. Notice how discreetly Edgar Cayce handled this description. The individual was at times mentally disturbed. Evidently, Edgar Cayce could tune into, on some occasions, action, location, and mental planning of individuals to whom he was directed without rapport created by a personal request.

On July 2, 1937, word was flashed all over the world that Amelia Earhart was lost. At 3:40 P.M. on July 5, 1937, upon the request of friends of both Amelia Earhart and her husband, George P. Putnam, Edgar Cayce gave a reading that indicated that Amelia Earhart was alive and personally in fair condition. Her companion, Fred Noolan, was described as suffering from exposure and in a state of fear. Their location was given as approximately 100 miles northwest of Howland Island. He indicated that the gasoline had run out and the plane was forced to land. On August 1, 1937, a further reading indicated that Amelia Earhart died on the 21st of July from heat and exposure.

In his book, *Amelia Earhart Returns from Saipan,* Joseph Davidson advances the theory that Amelia Earhart and her navigator were captured and beheaded by the Japanese. At least there is agreement on the theory that the two lost persons lived for a time after the crash.

The next case is in more detail and suggests communication between Cayce's mind and that of the lost person. On April 19, 1934, Edgar Cayce received a telephone call requesting information regarding the caller's father, who had taken a pistol and left home sometime during the night. On the following day the family had received a suicide note in the mail. The reading that was given follows:

M. D: You will have before you the [378] family, ——Ave., —— N. Y., in regard to the great trouble with which they are faced on account of Mr. [378]'s disappearance and the card which they received from him this morning, mailed from Reading, Penna., last night at 7:20, indicating that he planned to take his life; the last address they know at which he might have been, being 129 No. 5th St., Reading, Penna. You will give them all the necessary instructions and advice as to how they can get to him, if possible, and just what they should do. We seek this help in the name of Jesus, the Christ, and according to His will. Amen.

Mr. C: Yes, we have these conditions that confront those of the household, the [378] family.

In the affairs of individuals, through the activity of others and for the very faith that underlies those hopes, those aspirations of individuals, oft there come those experiences that seemingly cannot be borne. Yet each should know that He doeth all things well; that even that which is called impractical in the experiences or minds of some ye must do; ye must love one another, even thine enemies, even those that would do thee wrong. Know that God is in His holy temple, and those experiences that come to all must make our own lives, our own portions of Life or God—that we are experiencing—those things necessary for us to become less and less selfish in our motives, in that which would motivate our purposes, our ideals, our ideas respecting that others have had to bear—or as to what others have done respecting that they were called on to bear.

For, would we be forgiven, we must forgive. Would we have mercy, we must show mercy in our own lives, even though there may be felt in the consciousness of self that there has been little mercy; when there have been the greater attempts, the greater trials, to be of help and aid to others. And these very activities often, misconstrued, bring into the experiences of those so trying, slurs, unkindnesses said here and there—those that look and behold not the beauty in that which has motivated those attempts on the part of self to learn more of the Father's ways with His children.

Keep thine heart in the way thou knowest, that He doeth all things well. No burden, in this mind, becomes too hard to bear. See not the burden, but rather be able to give expression that the ways may be made the less tempestuous for those that are weary in bearing those burdens that seem too heavy to be borne.

For, believe ye in Me, that as ye ask in my name, that may the Father do, even unto those things that there may be yet the greater glorification of the Father in the minds and hearts and souls of those that are in turmoil, that age so burdened just now.

In seeking to communicate, only through those channels that have been and are of the regular nature or order may this be done speedily—as it has in part, and then—bear ye one with another. Seek peace in Him, that ye faint not; but that the joys of His love, His strength sustain thee, as He has given that they would in the hours of trial, in the hours of pain, in the hour of suffering. For, his love faileth not to sustain those that put their trust in Him. And though He slay thee, though He break thee as flax on the wheel, though He bestir thee to the depths of despair, know thy Redeemer liveth—and thou shalt see Him, and He shall purify thee in those things that thou doest that are lovely unto thy fellow man.

Those that bring for any contention and strife in feelings of resentment, either here or in those things that must shortly come to pass, will only close those views of His love making thee whole in thine own experience.

Then, seek in that channel through the offices that are for such purposes; and know that He can sustain in the hours of trial, even for Him, just now.

Ready for questions.

Q-1. Can you give more explicit directions—
A-1. (Interrupting) No more is asked by those in authority, and those only may seek—under the circumstances, through those in authoritative positions. See?
Q-2. Do you indicate the body is still living?
A-2. This should not be sought, just now. We are through for the present.
. . . 378–18

Other readings followed, one each day. None contained any information about the lost person that could be checked until April 23, 1934, when "Philadelphia" was mentioned. On April 24, the reading included, "the cough is bad." On April 26, it was stated, "it is alive —the body." When Edgar Cayce awakened from the reading on the 26th, he said that he had seen water and woods. On April 28, it was given that "there has been a communication penciled by Mr. X to the family. This should be received the present day or Monday." On April 29, the reading contained the admonition: "Rise, make known unto the Lord what thou wouldst do. The mind will clear in Him. Face the light. Draw near to Him. We see the body. Still in body." On May 3, the reading indicated "lots of water about the body this morning."

An encouraging note was sounded on May 12 when the reading included, "Everything much lighter about the body, about the activities of same in the present." On May 14, the following was noted, "Quite a lot of green about the body; more spiritually coming into the understanding of self."

A strange statement was included in the reading on May 21. "The physical body lives still among things green and yet it is the city of those that are called dead." Possibly the man was in a graveyard on this date. On June 9, the reading mentioned "Much grain about the body in fields." Then, on June 11, the following was included, "More hopeful—better conditions." And finally on October 1, a letter from the lost man was enclosed in the wife's letter of appreciation to Edgar Cayce. The man gave up the idea of suicide and returned home voluntarily. The readings were never confirmed point by point; however, the overall outline was confirmed and letters of appreciation for the help and encouragement given in them continued throughout the life of both the husband and wife. The man lived for 26 years after that.

Apparently, Edgar Cayce was able to contact the mind-body of an individual and trace his movements and activities. He was also able to determime whether it was best to give encouragement and enough details to reassure without giving information that would have enabled the family to make a direct connection with the individual until he was ready to come home. Also, it seems possible that Edgar Cayce undertook to telepathically impress the mind of the troubled man with constructive, spiritually oriented thought forms during the period of the readings and he certainly urged members of the family to pray and hold constructive thoughts about the father who had disappeared. The cough was bad, the pencilled letter did arrive, he was in the graveyard on the day indicated, and yet no detailed location was ever given.

For us, this is a most interesting study. More questions are raised than answered. Was Edgar Cayce in almost daily telephathic-clairvoyant contact with the lost man? Did he perceive this in an out-of-body projected state of consciousness, i.e., actually in consciousness moving to the graveyard, or to the place where the man was writing the letter with a pencil? Or could he have been picking up the actions, moods, and thoughts from a world of thought forms created by a troubled man's mind? If you recognize the possibility of this latter suggestion, then such patterns could be right at one period and then changed at another. It becomes very important to understand the time dimension in which a psychic operates, and it becomes increasingly clear that time as we know it—past, present, and future—exists only relatively, perhaps in relation to the point of observation.

In the next case of a lost person, perhaps the most famous kidnapping case of our time, the Lindbergh child, Edgar Cayce seemed to have been completely inaccurate. A friend of Edgar Cayce, David E. Kahn, got in touch with a friend of the Lindberghs and a reading was requested.

The following suggestion was given to Edgar Cayce on March 9, 1932: "You will have before you Charles Augustus Lindbergh, Jr., who about 7:30 P.M. on March 1, 1932, was removed. Give exact location of this body at this present hour, March 9, 1932—describe surest and best way to restore the child unharmed to parents."

The reading indicated that the child was removed from the bedroom by a man at about 8:30 P.M. Another man took the body. There was a third person in the car. It was further stated that the child was taken to a house in a mill section near New Haven. A section called Cardova was mentioned. Schartest Street was spelled out, and the house was described as a two-story shingle building, once painted green, but now brown. There were three men and a woman in the house with the child. The woman and one of the men were named. The child's hair had been cut and dyed, according to the reading.

Attempts to locate the area failed. On March 10, another reading was given that spelled out Cardova and gave further directions that seemed explicit enough. However, the directions were inadequate when attempts were made to visit the area.

On March 12, 1932, Edgar Cayce wrote to Dave Kahn, "Of course, I was not surprised when you asked about the reading for the baby. I have always had my doubts about anything very authentic on such matters unless it came of itself through individuals deeply concerned."

Further information was requested on March 12, 1932, when another friend of Colonel Lindbergh, became involved. Cardova was described as related to a manufacturing area including leather goods, shoes, boots, saddles, and the like. An entrance to mills was described and the house located in relation to this description. Adams Street was mentioned and the fact that numbers and names had been changed. This seems to suggest that Edgar Cayce was functioning in another time sequence.

Another reading was requested on March 13, 1932, and was given. This included further reference to Adams Street and a question was asked about it and answered. "In going out Adams Street, do you turn right at the first red shale?" (This seemed to be a confusing question.) However, Edgar Cayce answered: "Turn right at new macadam road on half street before end of Adams, two-tenths of a mile."

Apparently, Dave Kahn and Lindbergh's friend were unable to locate the house. And on March 17, 1932, a reading indicated that the child had been moved to Jersey City. The boy was not well.

On March 26, 1932, Dave Kahn wrote a letter to Edgar Cayce that said in part: "We found Adams Street after no one had ever heard of it. The city engineer only named it two weeks before."

The matter was dropped until December 20, 1935, when a reading was requested by a New Jersey government official through David Kahn.

A reading suggested that Hauptmann was only partly guilty. The following letter was written on December 30, 1935, to the official.

Dear Sir:

The special delivery letter containing questions on the case under consideration was received this morning and the information contained herein was obtained.

Through years of experimentation we have found it most advisable to set up as nearly as possible the direct contact between one seeking information through this channel and the psychic. Too, we are naturally concerned in making the proper attunement over the effect on the psychic resulting from mental contact with conditions such as surround this case. The above is given in order that you may understand just why the first approach was made in this manner.

In simple words the inclosed reading may be briefly stated as follows:

Hauptmann is only partially guilty of this crime. If the proper officials will eliminate any element of curiosity in seeking information of this nature, if they will take the responsibility in following the leads given though they may bring criticism from many quarters, help may be received through this channel in clearing up this situation.

As an organization we are interested in studying and checking all types of psychic information, especially those as manifested through this particular channel. The psychic is personally interested in being of help and aiding in any way possible in seeing that "the truth" is brought to light in this situation. We must insist that no publicity be given regarding any connection with this case—regardless of the outcome.

A second request for information direct or through Mr. Kahn will signify an understanding and agreement to the propositions contained in the inclosed reading and will receive immediate attention. The questions already on hand will be included.

We are most desirous of being of help but appreciate the tremendous responsibility involved and so ask that you give this angle careful consideration.

Yours very truly,

ASSOCIATION FOR RESEARCH AND ENLIGHTENMENT, INC.

HLC   Hugh Lynn Cayce, Mgr.

Nothing more was heard from the New Jersey official.

How could Edgar Cayce have been so inaccurate in giving information on this case? Let us assume for a moment that because of the lack of direct contact with the parents, the first reading picked a pattern of thought forms of people who planned the kidnapping but who never followed through because of the death of the child at the time of the event. In other words, Edgar Cayce in this instance did not tune into the event, only to the thought plans for it which were distorted. Many people believed that Hauptmann was not alone in the kidnapping plot. Certainly the fear patterns of others who were involved would distort the thought world that had to be penetrated by a psychic seeking attunement with the events on that fateful evening. Mental static must be very heavy in such circumstances. Only the most direct contact related to the best of purposes from both the seeker and the psychic can bring even reasonably satisfactory results. How different this world of thought forms of hate, fear, worry, cross-purposes, greed, and ego drives must be from that of a suffering person requesting a physical reading from a psychic who desires to help at a personal level.

CHAPTER 6

Readings for the Dead

The insistent ringing of the phone sounded above the boisterous northeast wind. Edgar Cayce's secretary finally reached the persistent instrument. "Gladys," said a voice, "Mom received R's reading and R was in her grave at the time the reading was given. I think I know what happened. Tell Edgar I will explain it to him when I come down the week of the 9th."

I imagine that call shocked Gladys like a shower of ice water. If the patient had been dead at the time of the reading, why didn't Edgar Cayce say so? Why didn't he know about the woman's death? Why did he give a physical reading when it could be of no use? Surely these thoughts flashed through her mind. Surely, too, ever since that day, these same questions have occurred to others.

If it can be shown that Edgar Cayce gave a reading for a person a day or even an hour after they were dead, skeptics will scoff, "Well, there certainly can't be any value in Cayce or his readings; if he couldn't tell that the patient was already dead, how could he tell anything useful about the patient's condition?" Others who have seen suggestions from readings applied to patients and have seen these patients improve will be bewildered by this incongruity. How could Cayce be so right in some readings and in others so wrong? In the file of over 14,000 readings, I found five cases in which readings were given for persons who were dead or dying at the time of the reading.

CASE I

Mrs. C: You will go over this body carefully, examine it thoroughly, and tell me the conditions you find at the present time; giving the cause of the existing conditions, also suggestions for help and relief of this body. You will answer the questions that may be submitted, as I ask them:

Mr. C: Yes.

Too late in the application of those things for material benefits in this present experience. As is indicated, not only the toxic forces have been the more active but sepsis has already begun.

These then would rather be for those who are mindful of the associations and relations:

Know that life is a continuous experience, and as there is a consciousness in sleep that is not physical—in the sense of physical awareness—so there is a consciousness in the same manner when the physical is entirely laid aside.

HE indeed is the resurrection and the life. In HIM do we put our trust.

Then there should not be sorrow and sadness in those periods when the physical turmoils and strifes of the body are laid aside, for the moment, for the closer walk with Him.

For indeed to be absent from the material body is to be present with the Lord.

Let those admonitions and those promises, then, fill thy life—and so determine within selves that ye will walk the closer with Him day by day.

And then when the shadows, as here, begin to close about, and there is the meeting at the river, there will be indeed no sorrow when this barque puts out to sea.

We are through for the present. . . . 1824–1

The family phoned—said they all felt it was useless; she is 82, has developed pneumonia—is ready to go, and all the children feel it is inevitable and have the right attitude, that they shouldn't grieve since she is happier to go.

Several points are worth consideration:

1. The request for the reading was made by the son of the patient, an A.R.E. member. Thus there was personal love and concern for the patient on the part of the person requesting the reading.

2. Edgar Cayce clearly stated that the woman was dying and that it was too late for medical help.

3. Some spiritual advice was given and accepted by the children, as evidenced by the report.

CASE 2

Another reading given five years later was similar:

Yes, we have the body; and the soul would take leave of same. *There are many experiences in a life's journey in the earth that are much more serious than that man calls death,* when the trust of the soul and heart of the man is in the Lord, who doeth all things well. There is little interpretation-physical of the disturbance, and it is gradually progressing in the inabilities of the entity to do for self, think for self. Even yet there is in the consciousness the desire that those, for whom the entity has been responsible for their being in the earth, should take note and prepare while they may to meet their God.

For the time cometh, as it must to this body, when no work is to be done but ye must stand before the judgment bar of thine own conscience, as must each soul, and determine as to whether in the light of the knowledge, in the light of thine opportunity, ye can as thy friend, thy God say, "I have dishonored no man, I have taken naught from my brother, but what I restore fourfold."

And remember, as this entity goes to its long rest, there are those whom he has entrusted with an obligation. Do not disregard the counsel. For he has been and is viewing those past opportunities that soon shall come no more in this life. There are the warnings, heed them! For the Lord will not always smile on those who disregard the warnings which have been and are being now, here, made to those whom this body would have heed the warning.

We are through with this reading. . . . 5195

This reading was also requested by the patient's son. Again, Cayce said nothing could be done and gave spiritual admonition only.

CASE 3

A third case again presents a request by a member of the patient's family, a father requesting help for his daughter:

GC: You will go over this body carefully, examine it thoroughly, and tell me the conditions you find at the present time; giving the cause of the existing conditions, also suggestions for help and relief of this body; answering the questions, as I ask them.

EC: Yes, we have the body.

There has already been departure of the soul, which only waits by here. We have the physical being but the control of same only needs the care, the attention, the greater love which may be shown in and under the circumstances, which will give the best conditions for this body. For already there are those weakenings so of the centers of the cerebrospinal system that no physical help, as we find, may be administered, only the mental or soul help as will be a part of the mental or superconscious self.

This condition has come from pressures which caused dementia praecox. We are through with this reading. . . . 8044-1

A peculiar reading, indeed; here may be a new definition of death. According to this reading the soul had left the body, which continued to exist in a state of insanity. (I hasten to add that certainly not all cases of insanity mean that the soul has left the body—that statement by Edgar Cayce applied to this person only.)

Again Edgar Cayce, as in the first two cases, recognized the hopelessness of the situation and flatly stated no medical aid was possible. These three cases certainly seem to indicate that it was possible for Edgar Cayce to tell whether a person was dead or dying.

CASE 4

The next case is a little harder to understand. On April 7, 1934, the New York *American* carried an article about a child, Theodoria Alosio, who was dying of leukemia in a Jersey City hospital. The newspaper also carried a photograph of the mother comforting the child with a lollipop. A member of the A.R.E., no relation to the child, became interested in the case through the newspaper clipping. She thought Edgar Cayce might be able to offer some advice in a reading that would help the child. She must have communicated her idea by phone or letter, because on April 14, 1934, she wrote: "Mrs.————and I visited the Alosio family and feel the mother has an open mind. We hope you will soon give the reading. Send no copy to Dr.————, just two to me and one to the mother. She hopes her own doctor will take the case. That would be fine. We always have Dr.————in the background. Ask about diet please."

During this same period someone had sent Edgar Cayce some clippings from a New Rochelle newspaper dated April 4, 1934, about another little girl, Roma Garrett, who was also dying of leukemia, and suggested that Edgar Cayce try to help her.

On April 16, 1934, with the following people present—Mildred Davis, conducting the reading, Gladys Davis, stenographer, L. B. Cayce, and, of course, Edgar Cayce—a reading was given. It was given after a check physical reading for another person. Mildred Davis held the newspaper clippings about Alosio in her hand and gave the usual suggestion for a physical reading. Edgar Cayce repeated the name several times and began:

Mr. C: [He repeated name, Theodoria Alosio, about a dozen times before starting with reading] Yes, we find the experimentations that are being made with this body are at the present somewhat more hopeful than has been and is ordinarily found in conditions of this nature and character, in one of such stages.

Should there continue to be the decrease in the red blood count—don't make so *much* disturbance, but—we would suggest that there be first a minute injection to the body of the properties that tend to make for the drying of lymph. Atropine see? First make this injection—one-eightieth of a grain, hypodermically. Preferably make this in the area near the spleen.

In at least three to ten minutes after this is given, or during the period when it is having its effect, give a transfusion that is as near as possible what the normal blood *should* have been. See?

And immediately after the transfusion begin giving Atomidine internally, three drops four times each day.

Also, as the foods, give beef juice and the enzymes that carry the iron —or the Venacular (?) Ventriculin (?) vernacular (?), that is reduced in strength.

And we should save these conditions.

Should it continue on the improve from the present applications, forget it! And this depends upon whether one of the things as intended to be done today is done or isn't done, see?

Should there be the response, we find that *these applications would be the most effective for those with leukemia, in such stages of development—or ages.*

Q-1. What would you advise regarding diet?

A-1. Beef juices principally and the enzymes. Beef juices will make a very well balance, but keep those things that make for gradual building.

We are through with this reading. . . . 534-1

The reading was mailed at once. On April 18, 1934, a letter was received from Mrs. [255], who had requested the reading:

Just as the reading came, I was going to send you enclosed clippings, hoping thereby to prevent your giving it. But it is strange, is it not, that the reading did not say the child   Theodoria Aloosio   had passed on on Sunday (4/15/34), the reading taking place on Monday afternoon? Some day please ask for the reason of this—perhaps the child—but then I will not say what I think. I had no idea the time was so short,—well, God did not wish it to be that way. I had hoped to be able to do something worth while for your work, but it was not to be.

It sounds as if Cayce gave a reading on a person who had died the day before the reading was given. Yet the reading did not mention the fact that the patient had died. What happened in this case? To understand, consider these facts:

1. The person seeking the reading was not related to the child. She was interested in having Edgar Cayce do something spectacular and wanted a part in it. Note her request for *two* copies of the reading for herself, and her specific request about the diet, indicating an interest in this particular aspect of treatment.

2. Only the mother is mentioned as "having an open mind," as if

other members of the family may have been hostile to the idea of seeking help from a psychic. Note that the mother herself did not actively seek help from Edgar Cayce.

3. The doctor in charge of the case was not told about the reading; in fact, instructions were given not to involve him at all—he was not even to get a copy of the reading. It was evidently supposed that he would not favor any dealings with a psychic.

4. Gladys Davis Turner stated that there was some friction between her cousin (Mildred Davis, who conducted the reading) and herself at the time. Also, Gladys said that at the time of the reading she was thinking about the other little girl, Roma Garrett, *and hoping some information would be given that would help her also.*

5. The specific wording of the suggestion given Edgar Cayce is not recorded. *The newspaper clippings were held in hand and the reading followed a check physical,* just the reverse of normal procedure.

The date on the newspaper clipping was April 7. Possibly Edgar Cayce's unconscious focused on that date and on the child's condition on April 7.

It is possible that all of these factors had their effect on Edgar Cayce and the information received through him. At that time, though, the burning question in everyone's mind was, "Why didn't Edgar Cayce say the child was already dead?" This question was so disturbing that another reading was taken in an attempt to answer it.

M. D.: You will have before you the information given thru this channel last Monday afternoon, the 16th, regarding the leukemia case of Theodoria Alosio; also our material questioning as to why this information was given —since the child had passed on the day before—and why it was not told in the reading that she had died. Was the reading given on the child, or simply on the condition? Please explain to the satisfaction of all concerned. Was the information taken from the period of seeking, or from that very moment the reading was being given? Is this why we should always have a definite appointment for a reading, with everyone in attune and seeking? You will answer the questions which may be asked.

Mr. C: In seeking information through such a channel, oft has it been given as to what factors enter in. Not that we would excuse what to a scientific mind would be a gross error, indicating that little credence could be put in such material information. But if the proper consideration is given all facts and factors concerning each character of information sought, as has been given oft, the information answers that which is sought at the time in relationships to the conditions that exist in those forms through which the impressions are made for tangibility or for observation in the minds of others.

Consider this particular case, then: The desire on the part of others to present that which might, perchance, be spectacular, that made the impression or influence that—irrespective of facts—there must be presented that which would be of interest on such a condition. And, as indicated by that given, the condition—rather than the individual—was given as a basis for scientific or other experimentation. For, as was given, the test being given, should this prove not helpful, then this as an alternative—or for the next case —may be tried.

Hence we find this becomes confusing in the minds of those that have not comprehended what is meant to be given respecting such individual conditions.

Then, of what value is this experience in the minds, in the lives, in the activities of those that—in their desire to be of help—sought? And to those who surround this channel of information, as they desired to also be of help; yet to each this must be as a failure, as a condition when all things may be questioned in their own selves.

Then, as the channel has proven—and, as has been given, only when credence can be found—in the minds of those that experiment—may that credence be expanded upon. But *always* must it be in keeping with those things that partake of the spiritual life itself. There must not be those things that would make for any desire to laud or praise or what not, but rather in the attitude, "God, Thy will be done in me, through me." Not, "My brother do this for the Lord will, through what I have said, give thee strength." No. "The Lord bless thee, the Lord keep thee," for nothing may be done of ourselves, but as He, the Father, through the Son, gives, that may be helpful, hopeful and a *blessing* in the experience of all.

Ready for questions.

In the first place, the suggestion for this reading is confusing, for it poses not one specific question but several—all incorporated in a suggestion given Edgar Cayce for the reading. However, as I interpret the answer, Edgar Cayce said that the desire of the party requesting the reading was for something spectacular, some miraculous cure with which to confront the medical profession. He went on to say that the condition, or leukemia in general, was the focus of his subconscious, rather than the Alosio child.

A couple of questions were asked in the reading, and the answers offer insight into the workings of Cayce's subconscious.

Q-1. Why is it that at times it is apparently so necessary that a body be at a definite location before we can obtain a reading, while at others the reading is given anyway from the "vibrations" of the body surroundings, etc.?

A-1. The character of the desire, as may be learned in the study of DESIRE in the life.

Here we find many questions that make for the materialist to say (and rightly so), "Because there are the requirements of this or that, it becomes hokus pokus, monkey business, nothing worth while." Yet the desire of individuals, as given—that one seeking, whether it be from the spiritual basis of "Thy will be done" or from that of "I must succeed in materiality" or "I must know for myself," these make for conditions in the lives of all those about the body, or about the channel, or those about the one to whom such information may be directed; and, to be sure, *alter that which may be given.* For, Life, God, whether cramped or flourishing, gives forth that it has under the environ in which it is.

Understand that, all, as you approach for information. This has been given again and again. When there is a question in the mind of the seeker, when there is a question in the interrogator, when there is a question in the recorder's mind, *these* must influence that interpretation of that seen by the channel through which the information comes. For, the soul of this man, [E. C.], my child, goes out into that realm from which such information may come. And "may come" is as to "How readest thou?"

As I understand the answer to the question, the attitudes, desires, purposes, and motives of 1) the person for whom the reading was given, 2) the person conducting the reading (the one who read the suggestion to Edgar Cayce and who asked the questions), and 3) the recorder or stenographer (the one who recorded what Edgar Cayce said)—all of these people had their influences on the information Edgar Cayce was able to obtain and transmit.

The second question points up the attitude that was in the mind of the seeker (the person who requested the reading on the Alosio child):

Q-2. Is it best for this Work that such information be used for a so-called miraculous cure of a case that has been widely advertised?

A-2. As given, and as given then, that given for such conditions—*for it's the condition rather than the body for which this is given*—would prove helpful; as a basis that many another body in its own experience might gain the greater experience; if God wills.

We are through. . . . 534-1

Cayce's answer seems to reaffirm that the focus of his subconscious was the *condition* of leukemia, not specifically the Alosio child.

Though Edgar Cayce did not consciously remember his readings, he was told about some of them when he awakened. He was keenly aware of apparent failures and inconsistencies. He was anxious to understand, and for others to understand, the reasons for those inconsistencies, as he showed in a letter he wrote after this second reading:

Regarding the information for the little child, if I understand correctly the enclosed reading—and what Miss Gladys and them tell me that happened when we tried to get the first reading, it can possibly be well understood that the information was intended for any subsequent experiment that might be had with such a case and had little to do with the individual case. Possibly many would say we are trying to draw on our imaginations, but if the whole circumstance is put together it can be very well understood—according to the information we have had as to how and why information comes through this channel. We are enclosing what was gotten, then, so that you may be able to compare and draw your own conclusions."

As with the other illustrations in this book, you must compare and draw your own conclusions. When it becomes possible to try Cayce's suggestions in a clinic it will be known whether he contributed anything of significance to the treatment of leukemia.

CASE 5

To return to the reading that began this chapter—on October 7, 1929, Mrs. [106] requested a reading for her sister-in-law, who was seriously ill. At this time, the Cayce Hospital was still in operation and Edgar Cayce was busy giving readings for many patients who came there for treatment. Aso during those days, Dr. House, the chief physician for the hospital, and an old friend of Edgar Cayce, was very ill.

Note that the sister-in-law did not request the reading herself—there is some question as to whether she even knew it was to be given, because Mrs. [106] asked that the reading be sent to her.

On October 10, 1929, Edgar Cayce wrote to Mrs. [106] to find out if the woman could be brought to the hospital, because patients entering the hospital were given preference for readings. As he expressed it: "We are so overrun at the present time, that it makes it very inconvenient for many who need the information at once."

On October 15, 1929, the nephew of the woman replied: "It would be prohibited to bring her to the hospital until after a reading has been taken. The woman has been operated on and is in a very serious condition. The doctors do not hold out much hope for her, considering it only a matter of time. In the reading we would have to ask the question very specifically whether she is a case for our hospital."

At about this time Dr. House died. On October 22, 1929, upon returning from his funeral, Edgar Cayce wrote to the nephew: "We have so many and we are so far ahead with appointments—I don't know anything we can do but make them (the appointments) when they keep insisting and asking."

On October 30, 1929, Edgar Cayce gave the requested reading. *Mrs. Cayce held the original request of October 7, 1929, in her hand and gave the suggestion for a physical reading.*

Edgar Cayce began:

Mr. C: Yes, we have the body here, [144]. Now, we find, many are the complications with the physical forces of this body, and these are complications both in the functioning of organs and in organic disturbances. These have to do with the depletion of the strength and vitality as related to the functionings, yet the forces in life continue to operate through these physical forces, and were [if] the care and attention [were] given, much might be accomplished yet for this physical functioning body.

The blood supply shows the vital forces, as have to do with little that is assimilated. While the body is under stress when digestion takes place, assimilation is much bettered. While the organs work under stress, yet the light—or the life—holds out.

Now, to meet the needs at the immediate time, or for that as we find that would aid—we would give, or prepare this, and this as the medicinal properties for the system:

We would take 16 ounces distilled water. To this we would add:

Wild Cherry Bark	3 ounces
Sarsaparilla Root	1 ounce
Wild Ginger	½ ounce
Indian Turnip	¼ ounce
Ginseng (wild)	1 ounce
Prickly Ash Bark	½ ounce
Buchu Leaves	1 dram
Mandrake Root	½ dram

Reduce this by simmering, not boiling, to ½ the quantity. Strain, and while warm add 2 ounces of grain alcohol, with 3 drams Balsam of Tolu cut in it. Shake solution together before the dose is taken, and we would take half a teaspoonful every four hours. We would not awaken the body to give the medicines, but when the body *is* awake, give it.

We would also apply these of the *colored* lights for the body. The infra red, we would say, on a Monday. The nile green on Wednesday, and the ultra violet on Saturday. See? These should be applied for not *longer* than *two* minutes in the beginning.

Do that. Then, at the end of ten days, when the whole is begun, we would give further suggestions for the changes as may come from this. Will [If] the body [will] respond, much bettered conditions may be brought to this body of [144].

We are through for the present.

It was on November 11, 1929, that Gladys received the phone call described at the beginning of this chapter. Later that week the nephew did come to Virginia Beach and talk to Edgar Cayce about the reading. The following information was taken from notes in Glady's diary:

Edgar Cayce wanted to give another reading to find out what had happened —why the reading was given after the woman was dead. The nephew said it wasn't necessary because the whole thing was clear to him. He listed several factors that may have caused the reading to be given as it was:—

1. There was no definite appointment made or time set for reading—only a letter dated October 7, 1929, requesting a reading as soon as possible. In a sense this letter may be considered as the point of contact between Edgar Cayce and the patient since Mrs. Cayce, the conductor of the reading, held it in her hand when she gave the suggestion for the reading.

2. The patient herself did not request the reading—in fact, she did not know one was to be given. Obviously, then, there was no meditative or seeking help attitude on the part of the patient.

3. Edgar Cayce was emotionally upset during this period of time due to the backlog of patients at the hospital and due to Dr. House's illness and recent death.

4. The nephew stated that he felt the reading had been obtained on Mrs. [144] as of the time of the request, October 7, 1929. Of course, there is no way of knowing whether the suggested treatment would have been helpful or not.

This whole question of the effect of emotions and attitudes on the part of the patient, Edgar Cayce, the conductor of the reading, the one requesting the reading (when it was not the patient), the recorder, and others present seem to affect the quality of the information received.

Certainly Cayce could tell when people were dead or dying if the proper suggestion was given. Obviously Cayce could go back in time. Consider the 2,500 life readings. However, even in these, particularly when he was answering questions, it is sometimes difficult to be sure of exactly what period of time he was referring to in his answers.

Maybe a crude analogy will help. Visualize a flat, two-dimensional plane of infinite length and width. In this plane exists a flat, two-dimensional bug. Let this bug have a memory and a free will. The bug is crawling along in a sine wave pattern. You, a three-dimensional being, observe the bug and its motion. In effect you see the bug's past, present, and future, and you see it all at once. Assuming the bug continued its sine wave crawling you could even predict its future position at any given time. Since this bug has a free will and may change its motion, you cannot be sure of your prediction, but you could see every possible position it might occupy in its future and you could see those most probable to occur.

Suppose you could communicate in some manner with the mind of this bug. Suppose the clarity of communication between your mind and the bug's mind were a function of the empathy between the two and involved attitudes, emotions, desires, and thoughts of each. You might reconstruct the bug's past and present quite accurately and its future to some extent. However, the bug could never understand how you could view at once what to it is the past, present, and future. Obviously there would be a communication gap between the two minds, yours and the bug's, due to the different points of view.

Possibly Cayce's mind, in his unconscious state, was able to view the past, present, and probable future of one's life and communicate this information to the one seeking help and understanding through his psychic abilities. Do you see a similarity between Cayce's unfettered subconscious mind, free to probe time and space, trying to communicate information to a mind encased in our three-dimensional world, and the trying to communicate with a two-dimensional bug?

When incorrect suggestions were given, when selfish motives were involved, and when there were conflicts of attitudes among those present at a reading, then Cayce's subconscious was not focused in such a manner as to receive the best and most accurate information available, nor was he able to communicate this information coherently to the seeker.

CHAPTER 7

The Nature of Psychic Perception

We have already discussed Edgar Cayce's successes and failures in a number of areas. Before we go on to the exciting subjects of treasure-hunting and oil prospecting, it may be wise to write what we now understand about the nature of psychic perception.

The purpose of this book is to examine some of the factors involved in the limits and accuracy of psychic data. To illustrate how some seemingly reliable psychic source can produce what appears to be inaccurate data, we chose an outstanding psychic, Edgar Cayce, with whose work we were most familiar. A significant number of Cayce's psychic readings seem to have been verifiable and helpful. We purposely scrutinized the relatively few that seem to have been misleading or downright wrong. The idea was that from those readings that appeared inaccurate, as much or more may be learned about the limitations and validity of psychic data as from the many that were proven correct.

An obvious criterion of the validity of data of any sort is its source. Where do psychics generally obtain information? Where did Cayce, in particular, get his information? How important are the motives for seeking and giving psychic information in relation to its accuracy? The answers to these questions are, we think, the keys to how accurate psychic information is likely to be. Unfortunately, the answers are not simple. What makes them complex is that there is really no one answer because on different occasions Cayce seemed to obtain data from various sources. To compound the problem, several factors certainly determined not only the source, but also the manner in which Cayce contacted the particular source and relayed the data to be transcribed. What applies to Cayce may undoubtedly apply in some degree to all other psychics and the exercise of their abilities.

Unconscious memory. It is difficult for the average person to be aware of his own unconscious memory, much less that of anyone else. In 1958, Dr. Wilder Penfield reported to the American Academy of Science his discovery of detailed childhood memories unrelated to conscious memory. Persons under local anesthetic, whose exposed brain tissues were stimulated by an electric probe (pieces of their skulls were temporarily removed for brain tumor exploration), "remembered" by reliving—hearing, smelling, feeling—childhood events. Such unconscious memories had long been the subject of hypnotic regressions. The electric probe was far more impersonal than a suggestion, and a slight movement to another brain area would bring instant "living memory" of another event. Hypnotic regression had been suspect because of the known characteristic of the subject to please the hypnotist and frequently fabricate data, a common problem in conscious recollection of fish stories and golf scores.

We must consider the possibility that Edgar Cayce's unconscious mind picked up information and restructured such data in terms of his "readings" for those persons who were present when the information was given. But it is inconceivable to these authors that some of the information given could have been obtained in this fashion. Specific spinal lesions are not observable to the most carefully trained eye, much less a tilted stomach, a childhood accident, or a disturbed menstrual cycle. Yet, we must recognize that Edgar Cayce used his unconscious memory bank in relation to perception of a psychic nature.

In those cases where persons were not present, the data must be examined closely, for the unconscious observation cannot apply, nor can even computerlike fabrication of the unconscious account for all of the confirmed date that was given. Distance, 43 years of consistent work, the character of the man, reports written at the time, and continued verification of data in the readings tend to suggest the presence of some type of psychic perception.

Clairvoyant observation of physical data. Many readings illustrate the fact that Cayce's subconscious mind seemed able to move from wherever he lay on a couch, to the location of the individual for whom he was giving the reading. The readings abound with such opening remarks, as "What a pretty rooster in the yard" or "There's been an auto accident in the street" or "He is not here now; he will be here in a few minutes." "Yes, we have the body here, he has just laid aside his paper he was reading" (531). "Q. Is this body in bed? A. No, she is sitting in a large chair, talking to a man" (168). "Yes, we have the body here. We have had this before. She hasn't dressed yet, you see" (1713). No statements such as these were ever denied, and many were corroborated by the patients in letters written immediately upon receipt of the typed copy of the reading. Edgar Cayce had to know the patient's name and where he was located at the time of the reading. Whether the patient was in the room with Edgar Cayce or thousands of miles away did not matter. It was as if he were on the spot and could see exactly where the individual reposed awaiting a reading.

A couple of interesting questions arise. Did Cayce see the surroundings through the eyes of the patient by some telepathic means, or did he view the scene as an independent observer, like a disembodied mind in an out-of-body experience. The facts seem to favor the latter, for he sometimes described a room where the patient was supposed to be but wasn't, or described an object outside the room that might not be in the patient's line of view.

There are also numerous references in the readings that suggest an out-of-body type of projection. On more than one occasion, Edgar Cayce stopped in the middle of a reading because someone passed an object (for example, a piece of paper on which a question had been written) over the central part of his body. When asked about this he explained:

As has been crudely given, a hen may lay an egg but the shell once cracked or broken *cannot* be made to produce that it contains. When the thought, the activity that is being made manifest, is broken, that which is creative or constructive—once touched by thought or suggestion—is hindered, wavered, as to that it may bring to a manifested form. Hence the experiences that are sometimes held, or that may be held, by those that may witness or experience the transmission of that which is received or gained through this particular channel, may —*by the mere disturbing of the body that rests above the natural body* by other than the elements that have not taken bodily form—break the associations, the connections, with that source from which the records are being taken. . . . 254–68.

On November 17, 1932, after Edgar Cayce had been given a suggestion to awaken giving a life reading, he spoke in a low voice: ". . . may ye, in watching close, see the entrance again of the entity as the body lies here and in the seeking has it been drawn far from the vault. Watch as it hovers near and enters, as the light of the body." . . . 2126–1 Apparently, some aspect or part of Edgar Cayce had left the fleshly body and was returning. Those present unfortunately could not see.

One individual (853) questioned Edgar Cayce on out-of-body experience. "Do I actually leave my body at times, as has been indicated, and go to different places? Edgar Cayce answered: "You do." The next question, "For what purpose, and how can I develop and use this power constructively?" Cayce answered: "Just as has been given as to how to enter into meditation. *Each and every soul leaves the body as it rests in sleep.* As to how this may be used constructively . . . this would be like explaining how one could use one's voice for constructive purposes."

It would seem from Edgar Cayce's remarks and from the variety of out-of-body experience amassed through spontaneous cases of average people that there is considerable evidence for this type of experience and perception through it.

Another question, not so easy to answer, is what limited his view in such cases? Could he see the internal organs of the patient? Could he peer into the earth and determine geologic structures or see oil pools and buried treasure, or was his vision limited to ordinary physical vision? Arguments may be advanced for both views. Until there is more data available from out-of-body dreams and experiences, this question may remain unanswered.

At any rate, surely one source of Edgar Cayce's information was this clairvoyant observation of physical data.

Telepathic communication between Edgar Cayce's subconscious or superconscious mind and that of other individuals, living or dead. The reader would probably be happier if this source were divided into two parts, living individuals and dead individuals, for to communicate with dead individuals presupposes the existence of a soul or spirit that exists after death (and probably before birth). Consider first the physical readings. Certainly one's subconscious mind would know more about one's physical ailments than any diagnostician. All the cause-and-effect reactions of a living body, all the individual's memory, is available for study if one could just tap this individual's storehouse of knowledge. Edgar Cayce seemed able to do this. He describes the procedure in the following manner:

Then in seeking information there are certain factors in the experience of the seeker and in the channel through which such information may come. Desire on the part of the seeker to be shown. And, as an honest seeker, he will not be too gullible; neither will he be so encased in prejudices as to doubt that which is applicable in his experience. Hence the information must not only be practical but it must be rather in accord with the desires of the seeker also.

This desire, then, is such that it must take hold not only on that which is primarily the basis of all material manifestations of spiritual things, but must also have its inception in a well-balanced desire for the use of such information not only for self but for others. Then there may come, as for this body in the present, that which if applied may be helpful in the present experience.

On the part of that channel through whom such information may come, there must be the unselfish desire to be of aid to a fellow man. Not as for self-exaltation because of being a channel. Not for self-glorification that such a channel may be well spoken of. But rather as one desirous of being a channel through which the highest spiritual forces may manifest in bringing to the material consciousness of the seeker those things that may be beneficial in a spiritual and material sense to the seeker.

What, then, is the hypothesis of the activity that takes place during such an experience? It is not merely telepathy; neither does a beneficent spirit seek to do a service by giving advice, as some have suggested. For, if such were true at all times, there would never be a fault—if really developed spirits were in control. But rather in *this* instance is *this* the case:

The soul of the seeker is passive, while the soul of the individual through whom information comes is positive. As the physical is subjugated into unconsciousness the latter goes out, guided by suggestion, on the forces which are released to that individual place of the seeker. *And the souls commune one with another* . . . 531-2

Time and again, physical diagnosis proved accurate. Childhood accidents and illnesses were recalled. Mental and emotional problems were bared, as well as physical ailments. With few exceptions, the patients who followed Cayce's suggested treatments got results, often remarkable cures. This type of diagnosis by Edgar Cayce suggests a strong rapport between the psychic and the patient and indicates to us a telepathic communication between minds at an unconscious level. We believe many of the physical readings (approximately 60% of Edgar Cayce's work) comes from this source—telepathic communication between psychic and patient at an unconscious level.

Communication with the minds of dead individuals. On one occasion Edgar Cayce was asked this question: "Is it possible for this body, Edgar Cayce, in this state to communicate with anyone who has passed into the spirit world?" Cayce answered: "The spirit of all who have passed from the physical plane remains about the plane until its development either carries it onward or returns it here. When it is in the plane of communication, or within this sphere, it may be communicated with. There are thousands about us here at present." · · · 3744

This was followed up later with a question on this reply which brought the following:

Q. What is meant by "souls within this sphere may be communicated with by Edgar Cayce in the psychic state"?

A. Each and every soul entity, or earthly entity passing through the earth's plane, leaves in that plane those conditions that are impressions from the soul or spiritual entity of the individual. This then becomes the fact, the real fact, in the material world.

The body, Edgar Cayce, in the psychic or subconscious condition, is able to reach all subconscious minds, when directed to such by suggestion— whether in the material world or in the spiritual world, provided the spiritual entity has not passed entirely into another level. Then we reach only those radiations left in the earth's plane. These are taken on again when re-entering the earth's plane, whether the entity is conscious of the same or not. The consciousness of this movement and development must (eventually) be reached by all.

. . . The physical world, and the cosmic world, or the astral world, are one —for the consciousness, the sensuous consciousness, is as the growth from the subconscious into the material world. The growth in the astral world is the digesting and the building of that same oneness in the spirit, the conscious, the subconscious, the cosmic. We find, from one to another, individuals are retained in that oneness, until each is made one in the Great Whole—the Creative Energy of the Universal Forces as are ever manifest in the material plane. . . . 900—22

Since death does not necessarily mean immediate spiritual enlightenment, we can assume, we believe, that in at least some cases, Edgar Cayce was tapping the minds of dead entities, as in the readings on treasure and perhaps oil wells. The attunement with such minds was created, we believe, because of the mental attitudes, the motives, and the desires of those seeking the information. Both of us were involved in some of the treasure readings, and it is impossible to fully understand the fascination and excitement of "the search for pirate gold" unless you have been involved. We were just as responsible for the failures in getting accurate information as the others before us and with us who sought such information. It would be easy to say, "It wasn't right for Edgar Cayce or the work at that time." It may well be more accurate to say that suppose in dialing the AAA for directions to a specific city, in your excitement you get the wrong number. Be smart enough to recognize a six-year-old boy who answers and give you *his directions.* We and others may well have tuned in Edgar Cayce to inadequate sources and not realized it.

LEVELS OF CONSCIOUSNESS

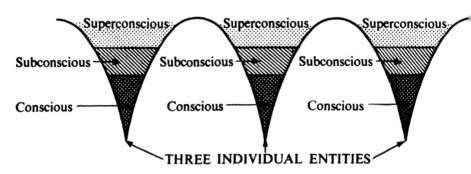

This diagram may be helpful in illustrating the levels of consciousness of individuals. The dark area represents the conscious mind; the shaded area represents the subconscious mind, and the light areas are the superconscious mind.

Applying the illustration to the physical body:

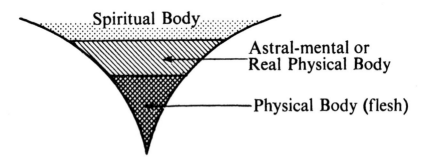

(Drawings used with the permission of Herbert B. Puryear, Ph.D., Director of Education, Association for Research and Enlightenment, Inc.)

Assume that each individual is made up of a physical body with a conscious mind, a mental body with a subconscious mind, and a spiritual body with a superconscious mind. Physical existence is confined to three dimensions and the conscious state, represented by the physical body with its conscious mind. Forming the pattern for the physical body is the "biological plasma body," a mental or astral body with a subconscious mind. This type of mind and body seems amenable to thoughts and suggestions. This mental body may be the vehicle of out-of-body experiences and the abode of the soul or spirit for a while after death.

The spiritual body with its superconscious mind represents the soul or part of God in every individual. This state of consciousness would mean an oneness with God and a loss of selfishness. From this state comes communication between man and his maker.

These three combined aspects of man—physical, mental, and spiritual—make up what Edgar Cayce called the entity or individual. If we are truly composed of such a trinity, we must surely view our existence here in a different light. Our conscious existence is only a narrow, concrete expression of man, in fact, one limited by three dimensions and not truly representative of our real spiritual nature as originally created by God. Once we move to the subconscious level, we must have a different view of time and space. It may be that (referring to the illustration of the two-dimensional bug) we could see our past, present, and probable future spread out before us. Maybe Edgar Cayce was able to obtain this point of view in giving his "life readings." In this world, thoughts may correspond to the physical objects and the "biological plasma bodies" may be the abode of subconscious minds both living and dead.

Now it is easier to understand that with such a different point of view and with so many varied sources of information, the manner in which Edgar Cayce was directed by suggestion largely determined where he made attunement. With his mind roving this different world, it is clearer why the suggestion for the reading was so important. And it also becomes clearer why the attitudes, ideas, and emotions of the various parties involved were important. From this point of view, it is not difficult to see why Edgar Cayce might relay data from an insistent discarnate entity who might be emotionally involved with the subject matter of the reading. Also, as in the illustration of the two-dimensional bug, it might not always be clear from what point in time Edgar Cayce was viewing the individual or subject of the reading. Many questions arise, such as how long does a thought last? What determined whose thoughts Cayce picked up? What determined which of the sources Cayce turned to in his readings? Did he sometimes draw upon more than one of these sources?

The answer to the first question is like the answer to how long is a piece of string. As to the second and third questions, there are probably several influential factors—the suggestion given for the reading, and the motives, attitudes and desires of all the people involved. Surely the mental, physical, and emotional condition of Edgar Cayce prior to giving a reading was also a factor. In most readings, it was as if there were some sort of rapport or empathy between the seeker and the psychic. Once, when someone was requesting medical aid, he inquired about a friend's ailment. Edgar Cayce quickly replied: "We haven't that here." Evidently, an orderly process of attunement had to be followed in order to get accurate results from Cayce's abilities —an attunement between Cayce's subconscious mind and the "inquiring mind of the seeker." Edgar Cayce seemed concerned for the growth of the seeker or patient—mentally, physically, and spiritually —as if reluctant to give more than the patient could constructively handle, feeling that knowledge not used is sin.

Generally, the best readings and best results came when individuals requested help for themselves or their loved ones with a prayerful attitude or cooperation and hope. In such cases, it seemed easier for Cayce to select the proper source of information that would be helpful and relay this information to the seeker.

In cases where general information was sought, the attitudes and motives of the individuals concerned were dominant factors in influencing the results. Cayce's mental, physical, and emotional state prior to giving the reading was important. Most of the treasure readings were given after losing the hospital—the wrecking of the dreams of a lifetime and the shattering of friendships that succumbed to greed. No matter how carefully worded, the suggestions for locating buried treasure must have been motivated by some feeling of greed, selfishness, or personal aggrandisement. Evidently these underlying motives influenced Cayce subconsciously in seeking a source. Perhaps they made it easier for external influences to manifest, a discarnate spirit perhaps. Possibly, they distorted his observations in time and space much like static may garble a radio transmission or distort a television picture.

The questions asked in many of the readings sound inane when looking back on them; many got the answers they deserved. Then, too, the fact that Cayce could move his subconscious mind so quickly in time and space made it doubly hard to phrase questions so that one knew for certain from what point in time Cayce might answer. Thus not only the source, but the factors that influenced Cayce toward a particular source also become important in evaluating the validity of the data received.

On September 7, 1933, Edgar Cayce gave a reading from the following suggestion: "You will have before you the psychic work of Edgar Cayce, and the enquiring minds of those present in this room, in relation to the phenomena manifested through him. You will answer questions regarding the phenomena, and such philosophical subjects that may be presented for explanation through this channel."

The information that follows clarifies and summarizes our discussion of the way in which attunements were made in various types of readings given by Edgar Cayce.

The answer to the first question constitutes the major portion of a ten-page single-spaced typed reading that lasted an hour and ten minutes. There are a few major statements and a summary of some of the other especially pertinent sections of what we think is an extremely interesting document from a psychic on his own perception.

Q. "What was the cause of not being able to obtain [355]'s Life Reading on Saturday morning, June 10th, when attempted?" The need for a review of how information was obtained was pointed out and the suggestion was made that laws were involved in making contact for such information. The reading then goes on to make the point that in previous incarnations the entity now known as Edgar Cayce developed the ability to function in "the realms of psychic or mental forces." It was also suggested that spiritual development related to such abilities had taken place on the various planes between incarnations. The reading continues:

Then, consider also that which has been given, that through the subconscious or superconscious forces of the entity the manifestations may take place; or from the superconscious or subconscious forces of entities that may have passed into that designated as the spiritual realm. Through these, or through the universal consciousness or cosmic consciousness from the very abilities of the entity Edgar Cayce to wholly subjugate the physical consciousness as to allow the use of physical organs that may be attuned to all realms that pertain to psychic or mental or spiritual influences in the realms about the entity.

The total dissociation from physical consciousness during a reading seems important. It continues:

Then, that which wavers or hinders or repels or blocks the activity through this channel when in such a state may be from these causes; namely:

The unwillingness of the body-consciousness to submit to the suggestion as pertaining to information desired at that particular time. Or the activity of the physical in such a manner as to require the influence or supervision of the superconsciousness in the body, or ill health, at such a period. Or the mental attitude of those about the body that are not in accord with the type, class or character of information sought at that particular time. Or there may be the many variations of the combination of these, influencing one to another, as to the type, class or real activity of the entity or soul that seeks the information.

For, as may be surmised from that given, one that would approach the sources of the information with the innate and manifested desire that that which is supplied in information should emanate from a loved one in the spiritual realm, and that desire has kept such an entity in the realm of communication, and there are those combative influences in the experience of that entity so seeking, and the development of the entity of the channel or medium through which the information may be attempted is capable of such contact, is there not—as presented in Holy Writ—the continual warring with the flesh and the spirit? The continual warring also with the spirit or entity or consciousness that would control through such a period of information passing from one realm to another.

There follows here a good statement on "as above, so below."

For (for further explanation), this should be known to all: The material realms or earth activities are as a shadow or a manifestation of a spiritual law, that may in its essence—when viewed from the realm of psychic or spiritual or mental influence—appear to be quite different; yet one is the shadow of the other. But in describing, then, as a shadow upon a material plane, there would be periods—according to the time of day, the position of the body from the source of light casting such a shadow—when there would be an outline that anyone would know that from which the shadow was cast. Yet at other periods the shadow would be, of the same body (material body), such that the description would not reach the consciousness of those even more intimate with the body from which such a shadow would be cast.

So, with that which may emanate through such a channel, there be many influences that have to do with the corrector of the shadow cast; remembering, too, that material things—or the vocal cords of a body, material—are being used as the means of transmitting that which may be seen of the actual or true body that is being described, analyzed, philosophized, theorized, or acted upon by or through that being sought.

Hence, there are laws that pertain to the activity; as to why there become periods when there is the inability of activity, or when the activity becomes hindered by *divers* reasons or causes, when they are so called in the material plane.

Edgar Cayce goes on to state that in the particular instance of the 355 reading, feelings in the room (where the reading was being given) make contact with the records impossible. The reading then asks: "How is the record made? How is the record read?"

In the material plane we have instruments that are so attuned through the raising of the forces in various elements of one or another of the consciousnesses that manifest in the material plane. As in the phonograph or the radio, or the prism light; or any of the activating influences such as in the stethoscope with its various acoustic arrangements for the activity of elements related to movements of various influences within the realm of man's activity in respiration, circulation, activity of contractings in muscular forces, tendon activities, ganglia reaction, and the like.

These are but, then (from our first premise) a shadow of the real realm in which the activity of life is recorded.

Then (to become more elucidating upon that we are presenting here), we must turn again to a first premise that we may make for the greater enlightenment or the cooperative influences that come to bear when these are in motion that make for a record.

For, as we see first in the material plane, to the material sense, (does) an object or a body that is called stationary produces the same character of shadow as one in motion. Far, far from same!

It might be even characterized by saying that an instrument for measuring time that stood still is correct in some realms twice each twenty-four hours, but never correct at any other seconds in that period.

(Just) so with the shadow of a stationary object; for that which appears even stationary is only relatively so, as related to or compared with that still in motion (through the sense stations of consciousness to a body in the material plane.)

Then life, or the manifestation of that which is in motion, is receiving its impulse from a first cause.

What is the first cause?

That which has brought, is bringing, all life into being; or animation, or force, or power, or movement, or consciousness, as to either the material plane, the mental plane, the spiritual plane.

Hence it is the force that is called Lord, God, Jehovah, Yah, Ohum (Ohm?), Abba and the like. Hence the activity that is seen of any element in the material plane is a manifestation of that first cause. One Force. And, as seen and stated above, a record in a phonograph is made up of elements of a certain combination of that which has become in manifested form in certain movements in relation to the first cause, for the projection (and does project) by natural laws; as the physical or material laws, then, are the reflection or shadow of spiritual laws. See? And these then make for, under certain laws, certain words, certain regulations, the retaining of that (through one of these elements or attributes of consciousness) which has passed before it; or that has been indented upon this element in this rate of activity of a first cause or first principle that is in movement, and unless in movement is not capable of being manifested in a material world. For, the movement itself (to make applicable another law) *draws* about a nucleus the positive and negative forces as to bring into visibility from one sphere or realm to another that force or power. Or it has lost that which makes for the raising or reducing of such vibrations as for the force, the power, the first cause, to become active in this or that or the other realm of consciousness.

Then, as the realm of record is made by indentations of other influences that act upon the medium that is used as the source, or plate, or manner of recording, so will there be—with the acoustic arrangements of that which is the negative of that influence which causes the indentation—*reproduced* that which has been indented by the positive activity upon that record, that plate, that plane, that activity.

So is this, then, as the record that is made of the force that manifests itself in the form of a body-mind with the attributes of all that vibration through which it has passed in reaching that place or plane of consciousness; It must be in accord, so that the record made is positive or negative (negative being error, positive being right—good!), that it may be penetrated to through the application of a negative influence upon that in whatever realm it may have made its indentation or record.

The reading then goes on to stress the importance of the purpose in seeking information. It is asked whether the seeking is in accord with the making of the record or is a seeking to correct the impressions or records made.

Hence, how easily may there be a diffusion or a break in that which may be obtained through such a channel, that is capable of attuning self so that it may write, read, hear, see, feel, or experience, and through *some* of the modes of approach to consciousness in a material world—give that experience which has been made by some activity; whether in this or that realm, in its course through that of eternity, time, space, or in the realm of the spirit itself!

For, as given, names but give metes and bounds to the consciousness of those that classify such activities in a certain stage or realm of conscious movement.

In the same manner we find the record as of the radio. The influences used here are simply a changed vibration of those very influences that have been described in their activity, and gather from this or that influence that which is being recorded. By the movement of what? The first cause, when in its activity in various forms or manners in a certain realm of consciousness.

What, then, is the variation from the one to the other? The reproducer of that recorded. In one it is required that it change its realm of activity for reproduction. In the other it is attuned to the first cause, that gives off in whatever realm or place that is attuned *to* the activity, the *immediate* response.

Hence, as from our first premise (the post), the conditions are only relative.

Then, the psychic influences or forces in manifestation in their various spheres are as but a type of needle upon the record; a type of acoustics in the recorded or de-recorded activity. Or the power and the influence by its development toward the realm of the first cause, as to the power of the tube or of the resoundant or of the length of its activity to care for its reproduction.

Hence, out of tune by many of the channels that have been indicated did prevent at that time [355] from receiving that later given.

A question was later presented asking why, when a life reading was attempted for 373 (who was born in Germany), only some words were obtained in German (a language that Edgar Cayce did not consciously speak). The answer shows again how much the thought of those present for a reading sometimes influenced it.

A-3. The attempt of one that might guide the thought of the entity seeking, that was of that speech only. You see where this fits in with that which has been given? Incapable of being understood through those present, then—*by them*—cut off!

Q-4. What is the interpretation of the German words given?

A-4. This is simply curiosity! Learn German!

Another question was asked about Edgar Cayce's memory after a reading of traveling to a hall of records in a bubble of water. At the hall he was given the books requested by a "keeper of the records." In commenting on this, the reading contains the following:

So, in the materializations for the concept of those that seek to know, to be enlightened: To the world, long has there been sought that as in books. To many the question naturally arises, then: Are there literally books? To a mind that thinks books, literally *books!* As it would be for the mind that in its passage from the material plane into rest would require Elysian fields with birds, with flowers; it must find the materialized form of that portion of the Maker in that realm wherein that entity, that soul, would enjoy such in *that* sphere of activity. As houses built in wood. Wood, in its essence, as given, is what? Books, in their essence, are what? What is the more real, the book with its printed pages, its gilt edges, or the essence of that told of in the book? Which is the more real, the love manifested in the Son, the Saviour, for His brethren, or the essence of love that may be seen even in the vilest of passion? They are one. But that they bring into being in a materialized form is what elements of the one source have been combined to produce a materialization. Beautiful, isn't it? . . . 264-68

Edgar Cayce approaches this explanation in a more symbolic way through a dream that he had during a reading period on January 15, 1932. Here is the dream as he described it immediately after awakening from the reading, followed by an interpretation given in a reading on January 25, 1932.

Saw myself fixing to give a reading, and the process through which a reading was gotten. Someone described it to me. There was a center or spot from which, on going into the state, I would radiate upward. It began as a spiral, except there were rings all around—commencing very small, and as they went on up they got bigger and bigger. The spaces in between the rings were the various places of development which individuals had attained, from which I would attempt to gain information. That was why a very low developed body might be so low that no one even giving information would be able to give anything that would be worthwhile. There were certain portions of the country that produced their own radiation; for instance, it would be very much easier to give a reading for an individual who was in the radiation that had to do with health, or healing; not necessarily in a hospital, but in a healing radiation—than it would be for an individual who was in purely a commercial radiation. I might be able to give a much better reading (as the illustration was made) for a person in Rochester, N. Y. than one in Chicago, Ill., because the vibrations of Rochester were very much higher than the vibrations in Chicago. The closer the individual was to one of the rings, the easier it would be to get the information. An individual would, from any point in between, by their own desire go toward the ring. If just curious, they would naturally draw down towards the center away from the ring, or in the spaces between the rings.

A. This vision is recognizable as an experience of the soul, or the *entity*, in activity. There have been various formulas or descriptions of how information for a body was obtained through these channels. There has been promised, through these channels, that there was to be a greater awakening to this entity in its field of endeavor. So in this way there is, as indicated, a way of the information being better correlated, better understood by individuals—who are through that as may be termed the attunements of the various directions, in the various portions of the country or world—of their relationship to the actual fact of seeking through the channels.

As indicated, the entity is—in the affairs of the world—a tiny speck, as it were, a mere grain of sand; yet when raised in the atmosphere or realm of the spiritual forces it becomes all inclusive, as is seen by the size of the funnel—which reaches not downward, nor outward, nor over, but direct to that which is felt by the experience of man as into the heavens itself.

As indicated in the rings, or the nets as of nerves, each portion of the sphere, or the earth, or the heavens, is in that place which has been set by an ALL Wise Creative Energy. Each may attain to those relationships by that which is attempted in the activities of an individual, a group, a class, a mass, a nation. In that manner do they create their position in the affairs of the universe. Each speck, as an atom of human experience, is connected one with another as the continuity of the cone seen, and in the manner that the nerves of an animating or living object bears upon that in its specific center, but reaches to the utmost portions of the universality of force or activity in the whole universe, and has its radial effect upon one another.

As the entity, then, raises itself through those activities of subjugating or making as null those physical activities of the body, using only—as it were (in the cone)—the trumpet of the universe, in reaching out for that being sought, each entity—or each dot, then—in its respective sphere—acts as the note or the lute in action, that voices that which may come forth from such seeking.

Then we find, in the classification, in the activity of those that correlate such information, those in the various spheres will naturally classify themselves—even as given in the illustration, that there will more often be the sound of help to those in Rochester than to those in Chicago. That only as an illustration. Not that there may not be as much healing to those from the one as the other, but the effect upon the individual in the environ makes for the tone which resounds from that received. See? This should, then, be a helpful illustration to those correlating in understanding and classifying the information that may be received. This should, to the body giving information, make known to him that there is being opened an access to the Throne themselves! See? . . . 294-131

The symbol described here is a cone or spiral. Edgar Cayce saw himself as a tiny dot in this cone. The higher the attunement, the broader the scope or range. The previous diagrams showing the body, mind, and spirit states of consciousness can be related here. The expanding top of the cone opens out to universal consciousness or awareness. The mystical experience is the result of an expanded awareness.

A world of thought forms This expanded awareness may be considered in another way, as suggested earlier. The stream of mind, the collective unconscious, the universal mind, the akashic records, or Edgar Cayce's world of thought forms may all deal with a world in which we are now living but of which we are only vaguely aware.

This is expressed in a variety of ways in the readings:

In giving the interpretations of the records as we find them, these are written upon the skein of time and space by the activity of the mental self. For the superconscious mind becomes the mind of the soul in those interims between material manifestations and the cosmic or universal manifestations —yet these are one. For it is as the activities of a day, of an hour—the reactions from same are dependent upon what has been builded in the consciousness of the soul. Thus these become, as here, a part of the whole entity's experience in the material sojurns. . . . 3605-1

In another reading, a direct question, "Explain from what sources this information may be obtained," brought the following:

Conditions, thoughts, activities of men in every clime are things; as thoughts are things. They make their impressions upon the skein of time and space. Thus, as they make for their activity, they become as records that may be read by those in accord or attuned to such a condition. This may be illustrated in the wave length of the radio or of such an activity. They (the activities, etc.) go upon the waves of light, upon that of space. And those instruments that are attuned to same may hear, may experience, that which is being transmitted.

Hence, do not in seeking confuse thyself that there may not be variations as to the interpretations of economic influences or forces that are being enacted in the thought and activity of varied groups. Just as either program may be sent from any given activity. The outer world is only an activity of the shadow world. . . . 3976-16

The readings are filled with references to a thought world which would appear to be as real, and perhaps more important, than our three-dimensional sphere.

For thoughts are things; just as the Mind is as concrete as a post or tree or that which has been molded into things of any form. And with their working abilities they may give to each of these purpose and activity that becomes constructive in the experience of all. . . . 1581-1

Hence the urge, as it were, to hold what would be called malice, and ever determining within self, "I'll get even with you yet." doesn't pay! for this only builds into self that held in thought—for thoughts are deeds; and become crimes or miracles! . . . 2071-1 There are the laws that are unchangeable, and that are ever creative and constructive in their influences. For, otherwise there are turmoils that overtake those who disregard same—that are unseen and not easily found by material reasoning. For, they are the results of thoughts. Know that thoughts are things; and as their currents run they may become crimes or miracles. . . . 2419-1

Cayce describes very clearly the world into which we move at death as being created by the mind. It is a world of thought forms, which can be a "heaven" or "hell."

What one thinks continually, they become; what one cherishes in their heart and mind they make a part of the pulsation of their heart, through their own blood cells, and build in their own physical, that which its spirit and soul must feed upon, and that with which it will be possessed, when it passes into the realm for which the other experiences of what it has gained here in the physical plane, must be used. . . . 3744-4

A direct question on this idea, "Are the desires of the earth plane carried over into the spiritual plane?" brought this answer:

When those desires have fastened such hold upon the inner being as to become a portion of the subconsciousness, those desires pass on. Such as one may have in gluttonousness, or in any condition that benumbs the mental forces of the entity. For the subconscious, as given, is the storehouse of every act, thought, or deed. Hence, as we have been given, all are weighed in the balance . . . We find these conditions become a portion of the entity to the extent that the entirety of the subconscious becomes imbibed with that condition, wherein the entity depends upon that element for its sustenance. In such conditions there are carried over. Hence the condition as is seen about such entity having passed into the spirit plane; it seeks the gratification of such through the low minded individuals in an earth plane. For as thoughts are deeds, and as such desire is loosed in the plane, such conditions become the taking on of the entity from the sphere, as is given, in that "thoughts are deeds" and live as such. . . . 900-20

Dreams, frequently referred to as "visions" in the readings, are in part, at least according to the readings, our perceptions of this thought world.

This has been builded by the mental forces of the body between the innerself or the subconscious self and the mental mind—that is, it is a mental image given back to the conscious body, the mental vision builded through by self and is then for the study of self in the mental way and not a physical application of condition, see? . . . 900-377

As this world of thought forms is built it influences the physical as well as mental and emotional activity in our three-dimensional plane.

Then a natural consequence—of how thoughts create those conditions that become as actualities in material forces. . . . Hence the lessons . . . as to how one in one's mental being may create those conditions that bring about just such physical results. But even as the visions are seen, these continue to be mingled together with both good and bad Just a thoughts create and bring about such conditions, then, desist! Either be on the one side or the other, and act that as would bring to self that desired. . . . 136-82

The concept of a world of thought forms is now new. However, it is strange to listen to a sleeping man who describes such a world as if he were a long-time inhabitant. In his unconscious state Edgar Cayce frequently expected those in the conscious state who were listening to him to be able to discern much more than they could.

It is possible to conjecture that the so-called dead comprehend our thought world more clearly than they are able to relate to three-dimensional bodies, and we surely sense their thoughts more easily than we can perceive the accelerated energy forms they use as vehicles or shells in this other plane.

Edgar Cayce seemed to be a traveler in many planes of consciousness. Like Marco Polo, his stories of what he saw seem improbable or impossible. Only in checking, testing, and making practical use of his data can we be sure that he was not a Baron Munchausen. Any way you look at it, the explorations ahead will be exciting, and we believe rewarding, as man discovers the true dimension of himself.

CHAPTER 8

The Elusive Treasure of White Hill

Q-4. What is the amount of the treasure?
A-4. This is sufficient to use the real effort for locating same! for it will be
more than a million—see? . . . 3812-6, April 9, 1931

These words spoken by Edgar Cayce over 37 years ago have caused
me personally some real efforts, like the back-breaking labor of shoveling sand from dawn to dusk, cajoling the help of friends with the lure
of pirate gold, begging and borrowing equipment that we couldn't
afford to buy. Were these efforts all wasted? Well, not entirely, but
let's not get ahead of the story.

It all began on April 9, 1931. A wheeler-dealer had been pestering
Edgar Cayce for several years with requests for readings on buried
treasure. Numerous readings had been given on various locations.
However, Mr. Prontes (this and other names used are fictitious) was
never content with just one location. If he couldn't find someone with
funds or equipment to finance one search, he would jump to another.
He was the sort who always had a lot of irons in the fire—oil acreage
here, a mining deal there, or some big development scheme designed
to make him rich.

Edgar Cayce condescended to give readings on buried treasure after
many misgivings, with the hope that the proceeds of what might be
found would be used to further his work. Then, too, this was after the
closing of the hospital after the 1929 crash and the shattering of Dad's
dreams of a lifetime. The family was in a bad way financially and

finding a buried treasure sounded like an easy way out.

Tales of pirate treasure have circulated around Virginia Beach for as long as I can remember. The area is rich in legend, since some of the oldest settlements in the country are nearby. Blackbeard, the infamous pirate, was killed at Oregon Inlet in North Carolina a few miles south. An old Indian trail leads from the ocean front to the Narrows and White Hill, through what used to be known as the Cape Henry Desert. This desert is anything but barren, consisting of alternate sand hills and swamps covered with vegetation. I am sure these spots were Indian camping grounds. One of my friends found an ancient musket wrapped in oilcloth hidden in a hollow tree near White Hill, and not far away another friend found the rusted blade of a sword sticking in a stump. More modern lawbreakers used the desert, too, for it was a favorite location for whiskey stills.

The desert was an admirable location to hide plunder, and White Hill, one of the highest sand hills on the bay, 59 feet above the water, was a local landmark. Legend had it that on or near White Hill Blackbeard buried a treasure.

On April 9, 1931, Mr. Prontes and two friends persuaded Edgar Cayce to give a reading to determine the location of any treasure buried on or near White Hill

Mrs. C: You will have before you the bodies and the enquiring minds of Mr. Prontes, Mr. Gray and Mr. Black, present in this room, seeking information regarding exact location of buried treasure on or near what is known as White Hill on Broad Bay, Princess Anne County, Virginia. You will give such information that will aid these three individuals at this time in locating such treasure. You will also answer the questions which they will ask.

Mr. C: Yes, we have the bodies, the enquiring minds—Mr. Prontes, Mr. Gray, Mr. Black—present in this room; also those conditions which surround the territory known as White Hill, or White Horse Hill, Princess Anne County, Virginia.

In seeking such information, location of same, much consideration should be given as respecting purposes, aims and ideals, as for the individuals.

As we find, there are—and have been—treasures, or moneys, jewels, papers and such, that have been put in this vicinity. These—*different* caches of same

—have covered various periods, and various experiences in the lives of individuals.

In and about the vicinity, over the same grounds, we also find where there has recently—today—been some explorations. In the west portion and to the south, the place where we would first attempt to locate same, or this first cache—the greater quantity lies there, as we find. Where the tree, that has died—but where there are indications yet of it having been a large tree, under the extended branches of same—in '42, as we find—the first quantity put there. Later in '61 there was another near the same place. These were put by individuals seeking to escape from their individual surroundings. We would seek out this portion or side of hill, using those aids and helps as may make for the indications and for the definite location of same. Do that. Ready for questions.

Q-1. Would it be advisable to use the electrical instrument for locating buried metals on this location?

A-1. That's just as given. Use same for making specific locations, for while there will be seen in the operation of same a confusion when the specific spot is to be located, but in the uncovering will be found that the *two* is indicated—as well as this once having been used as an Indian burying ground—see? will make some difference. The indications and the depths, and those things as necessary, may be followed *when* locations—and definite locations—have been made, as are indicated by the operating of the locater itself—see?

Q-2. Could this treasure be located satisfactorily from the gum tree which we marked this morning on the west side of White Hill?

A-2. Indicate this with the tree as spoken of, including gum—and around this whole area, see? using about ten to twelve feet southwest by south from this snag or portion of tree. This, then, will include the gum—see—to the west.

Q 3. How far is it from the water edge?

A-3. Well, we have many waters—and we have much change in same. Do some work to find anything, if you're going to use it!

Q-4. What is the amount of the treasure?

A-4. This sufficient to use the real efforts for the locating of same! for it will be more than a million—see?

Q-5. Any further information that would be of help?

A-5. Let's do something first—and then we may give more!

Q-6. Who is giving this information?

A-6. This from more than one, for there's been more than one indicated as have had to do with not only those of the natives—that seek that some changes be made—but the *general* information for those seeking same. We are through for the present. . . .

Note the opening statement of the reading: Edgar Cayce warned that in seeking the location of treasure much importance should be attached to the *purposes, aims,* and *ideals* of the *seekers.*

A few other points are worthy of note:

1. Evidently Mr. Prontes and friends had been to White Hill to look over the land and had marked a gum tree for reference.
2. They must have had some sort of electrical instrument to aid their search.
3. The reading indicated that several treasures had been buried there at different times.
4. The value of the combined caches was given as more than $1,000,000, certainly a sum worth some effort to recover.
5. An interesting comment was made about the source of the information. It sounds as if Edgar Cayce had been communicating with some departed pirates and Indians.
6. The general location was given as the south and west sides of the hill. The tree under which it was buried had died, but in 1931 a stump was left.

Mr. Prontes and his friends went back to the hill for further explorations the next day and upon returning obtained another reading:

Mrs. C: You will have before you the location known as White Horse Hill on Broad Bay, Princess Anne Co., Va., especially that part of it covered in explorations today by Mr. Prontes, Mr. Gray and Mr. Black, present in this room. Are the locations made this morning with the instrument, which we numbered one, two and three, correct? You will answer the questions which we will ask you regarding these.

Mr. C: Yes, we have those locations as made today in that vicinity of Broad Bay, Princess Anne County, known as White Horse Hill—this we have had before.

As is indicated by the indicator, or finder, these are *specific* locations—though not *all* that may be found in the immediate vicinity. That as called One, nearest the tree from which the indications were to be taken, this the deeper—yet one of the most important. While its outline is not as definite as number Two, that toward east or south and east, this—as we find—in *One* —would be that to be indicated or re-checked again. In *each* location the emanations are so different. In Three we find more decided, yet a much smaller area. This in the south and toward the west. This, as we find, should also be included. Do not, in the explorations, so handle that to be indicated or found as to *re*-handle in the various places. Begin first by re-checking the area. Outline these in a *definite* manner. Have sufficient either of those to *remove* same, by a rotation—that is, getting it out of the way—or use some piling. In the first, we will find near twenty to twenty-five feet. In the second, from eighteen to twenty feet. In the third, we would find some sixteen to nineteen feet. Ready for questions.

Q-1. Does that mean deep straight down or back in the hill?
A-1. Either way will be near the same.
Q-2. Would the bottom of that take it down under water?
A-2. To water *level* in some of them.
Q-3. Which should be gone after first?
A-3. That as indicated by the re-check of the most *definite* point—see?
Q-4. Is this hickory tree the right tree to start from?
A-4. It's better to start from the location than from the tree! The outline that is made by the indicator, *there* start—see? Outline same.
Q-5. Give specific instructions as how to recover it.
A-5. As given. Either use those of piling or make the area sufficient that this will not have to be re-handled—see?
Q-6. Will there be any difficulties encountered in digging there, from any sources?
A-6. We do not find it so, provided there are those precautions taken as natural and incident to such explorations.
Q-7. Any other information that will be helpful at this time, or any warnings?
A-7. *Check* first—*re*-check, see? Follow that one that is the most *definite* outline, see? Outline the area. Then give self-sufficient of an area to remove covering—see? We are through for the present. . . .
3812-7

Again some points are notweorthy.

1. Edgar Cayce did not give a *specific* location but left that up to Mr. Prontes and his locator.
2. The caches are buried extremely deep.
3. One clue that sounds helpful is that the distance to the treasure straight down or back into the hill is about the same; this would seem to locate it on the side of the hill where the slope is about 45° (see diagram).

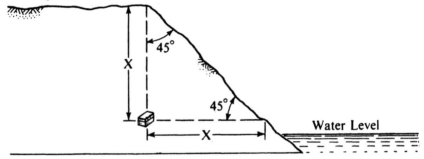

This point plus the extreme depth raises some questions as to how and why it was placed in such a location. Did those who placed it there tunnel back into the hill or dig straight down? In either case some sort of shoring, piling, or support would have been necessary to keep the sand from caving in. On the other hand, maybe it was not buried that deep at all, but the sand hill may have shifted so that it is now much deeper than when it was buried originally.

At any rate, the great depth of the treasure must have discouraged Mr. Prontes and his friends, for there is no record of further efforts on their part to excavate the locations.

I had been familiar with the readings on White Hill for a long time, but the extreme depth of the cache presented a problem in both location and removal. Furthermore, White Hill is located in a State Park. Any treasure-hunting would have to be done surreptitiously or with the permission of the State authorities. In addition, the trail to White Hill is not designed for automobiles. A four-wheel-drive vehicle can negotiate it, but an ordinary car would get hopelessly stuck. Since it is on the water it may be reached by boat, but only by one of shallow draft, as the depth of the water is only a couple of feet even a hundred feet from shore, and within fifty feet of the shoreline it is less than a foot.

Just getting to such an inaccessible place requires some effort, much less transporting equipment of any sort there. White Hill itself is very large. The trail coming in begins to rise a hundred yards or so from the bay, and when one bursts through the trees at the trail's end, the view from the top is magnificent. All of Broad Bay can be seen from the Narrows at the south end to Long Creek at the north. A good deal of undergrowth covers the hill and even some good-size pines. Pines grow rapidly, but on the southwest slope about one-third of the way up the hill is a large pignut hickory tree that must be 150 to 200 years old, judging from its diameter of 3½ to 4 feet. Just under the sand and fallen leaves are a maze of roots, as we learned later. The hill slopes gradually downward into a ridge of dunes to the north, but to the south it bends sharply around a swampy area that looks like the mouth of a former creek. Thus the southern portion of the hill is fairly well defined. Although sand dunes are known to move around with the wind, the amount and size of the undergrowth over White Hill indicates that it has been stabilized for a long time.

My first efforts were directed toward trying to obtain a metal locator capable of detecting a buried object at a depth of from 16 to 25 feet in sand. Of course, the main drawback to this was that the physical dimensions of the treasure container had never been mentioned. The information that there was more than one cache was helpful, and the statement that the total value was $1,000,000 or more logically indicated a large quantity of either gold or silver. Was the container metal or wood? Was it the size of a barrel or large chest or was it a small cask or box?

When I started my investigations I knew little about metal locators. (A few years later, *Consumer Research Bulletin* accepted an article by me on the capabilities and limitations of metal detectors.) I won't relate my futile efforts to obtain a device capable of detecting a 2 x 2 x 2 metal object at a depth of 25 feet. A few years ago no such device existed, and if one exists now, I am not familiar with it. Some manufacturers claim a range of 25 to 30 feet for their equipment, but to detect an object at this depth it has to be as large as an automobile or small house. However, I wasn't satisfied until I had tramped all over the hill with a metal locator. A friend of mine worked for the city and had access to one that was used to locate underground metal pipes. This was a larger and more powerful device than the ones owned by the utility company for which I worked. The manufacturer claimed a maximum range of 25 to 30 feet on large objects. Of course we didn't know the size of the object we were looking for, but we knew that if it was in a metal container that had rusted, it would present an effectively larger area and might be detected. Also we didn't know but what shifting sands might have buried the treasure deeper or even uncovered it somewhat.

Experiments on a freshly buried engine block in sand showed that we could get postive identification at 5 to 7 feet. A rusted metal container should be able to be detected at 10 feet or more if it were large enough. Anyway, we tramped over White Hill, over every foot of the "south and west portion." Our only discoveries were some rusty tin cans left by careless campers. Until you have trudged for hours in the sun, up and down and across a soft sand hill, around trees and through underbrush, carrying a 25-pound metal locator, you can't begin to realize the work involved. It is no longer a lark, but dirty, sweaty work.

While the results of this labor were disappointing, they were not conclusive. The treasure, if there was one, had to lie beyond the range of our metal locator. We then began considering other methods of attacking the problem.

Months later another scheme was tried. This consisted of using a "megger," or ohmeter, with a set of four steel rods to measure relative ground resistance between two of the rods. In this method the spacing of the rods is related to the depth of detection. The area in question is staked out and a great many resistance measurements are taken and plotted like a contour map. Presumably areas of low resistance indicate a conducting medium different from that of the surrounding ground and these particular spots can then be investigated by digging. This method may work well in dry, high resistance ground, but on White Hill it failed miserably. When the rods were separated by 20 to 25 feet the resistance of the sand permeated by salty bay water turned out to be very low. Salt water is a good conductor of electricity, so I do not think any metal located in a salt water sand complex is detectable by this method.

In the next phase of exploration, I dug very deep holes at random with an auger with the help of a fellow employee. (You would be surprised how easy it is to recruit treasure-hunters.) The auger we used was different from an ordinary posthole auger in that it had extension handles. One could add five-foot sections until it got too heavy to lift. The bit of the auger held about a shovel of sand. It took two of us 1½ to 2 hours for each hole. We dug three or four 20- to 25-foot holes, hoping to hit some trace of the Indian burying ground mentioned in the reading or some signs of old piling or a tunnel. We didn't see how anything could have been buried at that depth without some supporting structure to keep the hole or tunnel from caving in. But our results were entirely negative.

After this failure matters rested for a while. What we needed was a definite location, or a way of moving a tremendous amount of sand, like say, the southwest side of White Hill. A bulldozer could do it, but besides being expensive, it would attract attention. Further, State Park authorities would surely take a dim view of destroying trees and a natural landmark. A number of schemes were suggested and discarded, mainly because of the difficulty of getting any kind of equipment to the site.

One suggestion that looked promising was the use of a high pressure water pump. We would simply wash the sand away with a jet of water. The slope of the hill afforded a natural runoff, and plenty of water was available in the bay. We began working on obtaining a high pressure pump and some fire hose. Almost immediately our search was rewarded. The manufacturers of the Willis Jeep had just brought out a small auxiliary fire engine. It was a four-wheel-drive Jeep with a high pressure fire pump mounted on the front. Better yet, one of the Jeep salesmen was a young boy and a good friend of another of the "treasure-hunters."

It took a little persuading and involved cutting in another person on the "treasure," but one Saturday we had arranged for a demonstration of the auxiliary fire engine. Getting it over the trail was no problem since it had four-wheel drive. Getting it down to the bottom of the hill close enough for the 20-foot intake suction hose to reach the water was another matter. Fortunately we had brought another Jeep and some block and tackle. Three hot, sweaty hours later the task v is accomplished. At first the sluicing idea worked well, but soon several things became apparent: The runoff from the hill contained sticks, leaves, and roots as well as sand, and all this debris began to clog up the intake to the pump. The small 2½-inch hose gave good pressure at sea level, but when the hose was run 40 to 50 feet up the hill, the pressure was greatly diminished. We needed more hose. And once the top layer of sand was washed away a maze of roots was exposed. These had to be cut through with an ax or machete so the sluicing could be continued effectively.

In spite of these difficulties we cut a couple of deep gashes in the side of the hill and at the end of the day had moved more sand than a dozen people shoveling could have moved in a week. However, no evidence of old piling or tunnels or Indian bones or chests of gold was uncovered.

Getting the fire engine back up the hill proved even more of a task than getting it down. By the time it was accomplished, the Jeep salesman had had his fill of treasure-hunting. The rest of the crew were in a different frame of mind. We saw the possibilities of a larger pump and more fire hoses. Why, we could literally move mountains. We also realized the next expedition would require more planning.

First, with the help of a friendly politician, we obtained permission from the State Conservation Commission to look for Indian relics in the State Park. This letter also authorized minor excavations.

Next we set about procuring a larger pump and more fire hoses. A volunteer fire department provided both. They had what was known as a civilian defense fire pump, which consisted of a 140 hp. Chrysler gasoline engine and a 500 gal./min. pump mounted on a trailer. This pump could serve one four-inch hose and one two and a half-inch hose simultaneously. The equipment was really a World War II relic and was seldom used. It was not too difficult to borrow it along with a quantity of fire hose. All we had to do was promise to clean up the pump and hose before returning it.

We knew it would be a difficult job getting the heavy trailer over the trail and down to the bottom of White Hill, but we were young and enthusiastic, and by then had some experience in such matters.

One Saturday at daylight we started. By 10:00 A.M. the trailer was in place at the bottom of the hill. This time we were more cautious. The water intake had a filter and the trailer was situated so that the runoff did not run so near the intake. The four-inch hose was very effective, and it was all one person could do to hold the hose and direct the stream of water. By nightfall we had a hole in the hill big enough to bury a house, and by Sunday noon we had cut a deep trench across the southwest side. Sunday night found four weary, sunburned treasure-hunters assessing the project. We had found how to dig a big hole in a sand hill, but we had found no treasure. Of course, we had been "digging in the dark" without a specific location, but we were discouraged. Without a definite location we all felt further excavating would prove fruitless.

For a year or so no more digging took place on the hill. The trenches and holes gradually filled up with loose sand and a new sand bar appeared off shore. I kept writing to manufacturers of metal detectors to keep abreast of current developments. The trend then, though, was toward lightweight equipment and the development of a waterproof locator that could be used underwater to pick up metallic objects on the ocean floor. No one made a better locator, that is, one with a longer range, than the one we had already tried unsuccessfully. We even obtained the use of an expensive magnetometer and explored the hill with it. We found a lost probing rod and some tin cans, but no treasure.

We had considered trying another psychic, but we didn't know of any who had been successful at treasure-hunting. Then in the early part of 1951, I ran across a book by Kenneth Roberts called *Henry Gross and His Dowsing Rod,* which told of the remarkable abilities of Henry Gross, a dowser. (A dowser is one who can locate water by walking over an area with a forked stick. Over underground water this forked stick twists, or so the dowsers claim, and points down toward the water.) The interesting part of this book was not only Mr. Gross's successful location of underground wells and streams of water, as testified to by numerous disinterested parties, but his ability to dowse from a map. As related in the book, Mr. Gross could take a map, go over it with his dowsing rod and mark areas where water might be found. Upon going to these same spots in the field, his dowsing rod again would indicate water, and upon digging, water would be found. His success after hundreds of trials indicated to me that here was a man with definite psychic ability. Another point that intrigued me was that besides finding water, he had located one or two lost objects, one of them being an outboard motor. If he had ever tried to locate buried treasure, it wasn't mentioned in the book. However, the possibility that he might be able to do just that seemed worth pursuing further. Thus began a lengthy correspondence that culminated in our last expedition to White Hill.

On May 7, 1951, I wrote to Mr. Roberts and Mr. Gross as follows:

Doubtless you receive many such letters, but I hope the peculiar facts of this one merit your attention and interest.

[Here I gave a brief background concerning myself and my father, Edgar Cayce.]

It was necessary to go through the above preamble to show you why I am writing you. I have just read the book on your amazing dowsing ability, and I would like you to engage in an experiment with me.

In one of my father's "readings" there is a reference to some buried pirate treasure (probably consisting of gold, silver, monies or papers) buried in a sand hill in this county. The directions were given from a stump that we have been unable to locate, though the hill, a large one, was found. The depth of 16 to 20 feet is beyond the range of present day mine detectors or metal locators. The location of the hill is such that it is not practical to tear it down with bulldozers.

What I propose to do is to send you maps and photographs of the hill. If you get answers that indicate you should be on the spot, the expenses of the trip could be arranged. Whether you come or not, I would agree to divide anything found with you on a 50–50 basis (I would stand all expense of excavation).

Hoping to hear favorably from you, I remain

Sincerely,

Edgar Evans Cayce

Because over a month had gone by since I first wrote, I was beginning to despair of hearing from him at all. Then on June 28, I received a reply:

Dear Mr. Cayce:

Our chief concern is water. Mr. Gross has had plenty of experience on that, and we know he's accurate.

Just so you understand that we make no claims concerning Mr. Gross' ability to find anything but water, go ahead and send your maps and photographs. We'll take a shot at them without any fee involved. If anything develops from it we'll start all over again.

Sincerely,
Kenneth Roberts

His letter filled me with renewed hope. To give him all possible cooperation, I procured an aerial photograph of White Hill and had it enlarged. Also, because fortunately one of the members of our treasure-hunting crew was a licensed pilot, we flew low over the hill in a light plane and took a number of pictures. All of this material together with a map of the area was mailed to Mr. Roberts.

Within a week we received an encouraging reply from Mr. Roberts:

Dear Mr. Cayce:

I'll have to say again that Henry has had no experience in matters of this sort. We're willing to take a chance on it, though, because we know of your father's remarkable work—and because you obviously are as disinclined to publicity as we are. The boys who cover dowsing stories just can't seem to get things right.

Henry's rod tells him that there are four buried boxes on the area indicated in your photographs. None of the snapshots give all four of these. Before using his rod on the photographs, he touched a rod to a George II silver pitcher. I used a razor blade to cut the cross marks, so they'd be as accurate as we could make them from a distance.

We have marked the four boxes on the aerial photograph. So far as Henry could tell, there is no indication of any Indian burying ground on any part of the circled portion. Perhaps if we had had a dead Indian to touch the rod to, the results might have been different.

Three of the boxes appear on picture #7, and only two under picture #8 —though we're unable to say why there should be one more on 7 than on 8.

The box indicated on picture #3 seems to be 8 feet down, and the value of its contents *now* seem to be around $52,000.

Picture #6 shows a box at a depth of 10 feet, with a present valuation of some $30,000.

Picture #5 shows one box at a depth of 11 feet with a present valuation of around $60,000.

We can't place the fourth box on any of the snapshots, but we've shown it on the map.

I'm returning all the photographs and maps, and it's possible that from them you may be able to find out whether the rod is replying as correctly as we hope it is. We'll be very much interested in hearing your reaction.

Naturally, we were elated to find such close correspondence between two different psychic sources even though there was a considerable difference in the amount of the treasure.

Although we were anxious to try our new information, we wanted to be sure we were properly equipped and digging at the right spot. I wrote again explaining our difficulty in getting equipment of any kind to the hill and enclosed some additional pictures of what I thought were the areas Henry Gross had pinpointed on the previous maps and photographs.

The reply to this letter seemed inconsistent with the first information we had received, and we were somewhat nonplused:

Dear Mr. Cayce:

If there are any buried boxes on your land, they must be in friable soil. Since this is the case, why don't you sink test holes with a post hole augar?

In re-checking your photographs, the depths are considerably different from our original findings. 'E' now shows at 7 feet. 'B' now shows at 16 feet. 'D' now shows at 12 feet. I have no idea why there should be this variation in depth.

However, since we had all the quipment lined up, we decided to go ahead with the information originally given and the marked photographs.

We had made some improvements on our equipment. Instead of the heavy, unwieldy civilian defense fire pump we had obtained what is known in the Navy as a "handy-billy," a high-speed centrifugal pump powered by a 32 hp. outboard motor. It is readily portable by two men and the gasoline requirements are much less than for the 140 hp. marine engine. The output, though less, is still a respectable 250 gal./min. from a 2½-inch fire hose.

Also we had a quantity of 8-foot steel ground rods with which we could probe 6 to 7 feet into the sand. By washing away 6 or 7 feet of cover and probing over the area with the ground rods we could explore a large area approximately to a 12- to 14-foot depth. On August 4th and 5th we proceeded with our expedition as planned. We wrote to Mr. Roberts and Mr. Gross:

August 7, 1951

This past Saturday we tried excavating in two places on White Hill without finding any evidence of any buried boxes; the obvious conclusion being that we either did not dig in exactly the right spot or else did not go deep enough. [I then described our method in detail.]

The net result was that in the location on the side of the hill (the one that showed 7 feet deep your first try and 10 feet deep later (we covered an area about 8 to 10 feet wide and 15 feet long down 12 feet deep and a smaller area down 15 to 20 feet. On top of the hill (the one that showed 11 feet and 12 feet deep) we removed an amount of sand approximately 8 feet wide, 8 feet long and 8 feet deep and then probed in this hole another 6 feet with the steel rods (rods were driven a foot apart over bottom of hole).

Therefore with our limited time (all of the men participating work during the week and have only Saturday and Sunday for this searching), we proved only that there was nothing in the spot we dug; evidently our location or depth, or both, were off.

Of course, we plan to continue the search until we have removed enough sand to such a depth as to definitely establish the fact that nothing is buried in the area or until we find all the boxes.

Until such time as you find it convenient to come down, I shall keep you advised of our progress.

Sincerely,
Edgar E. Cayce

P.S. Regarding the soil, it is entirely loose sand; there are some roots down 4 to 5 feet and after that only sand which is, of course, packed harder the deeper you dig, but it is still loose sand with no trace of clay, rock or other type soil."

Treasure-hunters aren't easily discouraged, and we kept trying to get Henry Gross on the spot. By now both Hugh Lynn and I were anxious to meet him and see him perform. We wrote a number of times trying to persuade him to dowse White Hill in person. We also kept trying to get additional directions by mail from snapshots taken at various locations on the hill, but working from photographs seemed very unsatisfactory.

When we could spare the time, we dug in the locations Mr. Gross marked on the snapshots of the hill. We found nothing. Several weeks passed.

Finally, at my suggestion, my brother, Hugh Lynn, wrote to Mr. Roberts and Mr. Gross in a last effort to get them to try on-the-spot dowsing. (We had begun corresponding in May and it was now winter.)

November 9, 1951

I have followed with great interest your correspondence with my brother, Edgar Evans Cayce. I have gone over the "site" with him several times and on one occasion spent a day with him and the young men who are working with him assisting with the excavation.

He has asked me to write you with regard to a discussion which we have carried on intermittently in connection with ideas as to the source of the information and the various possible involvements in its transmission. I refer to both the information we received on this "site" through Edgar Cayce and also that you and Mr. Gross have gotten with the rod.

Let me hasten to say that this is being presented simply as a matter of discussion. As you will see it is an assortment of ideas approaching the subject from several different points of view.

In discussions with my brother and the young men who are working with him, this basic question has been examined. What are the possible sources for information on buried treasure and what are the complications which might arise in transmitting it? Psychic research in general, and this would include the work done with telepathy, clairvoyance, dowsing and spirit communication, seems to indicate that some individuals on the earth plane are possessed of powers of extended perception. Such perceptions operate through any one or all of the five senses. I have tried to illustrate this by saying that an individual sitting in a room with the windows closed and blinds down might be compared to an average human being.

Obviously if one could raise the blinds and open the windows this individual could see and hear more clearly what was going on outside. Conceivably an individual sitting in the room who was possessed of particularly keen eyesight or a particularly keen sense of hearing, let us say, would be able to discern more than someone with inferior sight and hearing. Our sensitive, therefore, is a person whose blinds are raised and whose windows are open at times. Clairvoyance we could then define as the ability to see what was going on at a distance, as clairaudience would be a similar ability of hearing. It seems quite likely that we might extend this sense of perception to feeling, to include dowsing ability. Psychometry falls more exactly under this heading.

Now if we move in another direction for a moment and postulate that some type of survival of personality is possible we have assisting in the area outside of our sensitive's room (his body, (a) thoughts and impressions of action of individuals who have passed on, and (b) actual personalities existing in some type of finer body. Now if our sensitive begins to perceive the existence of such impressions or personalities he becomes involved in what we may call spirit communication and reports not only what he sees and hears and feels at a distance in time and space, but also what is transmitted to him by personalities interested in the same subject he is pursuing.

Perhaps all of the above is just an involved way of saying that either with Edgar Cayce or with you we cannot eliminate the possibility that they are working with a clairvoyant power of their own inner makeup or with a communication with personalities existing in another plane of consciousness independent of them. I think it is quite possible that we may have to consider both sources of information at the same time.

I have told my brother that in my opinion you and Mr. Gross have come way beyond the explanations given in your book on his dowsing work. It is possible that you have formulated some specific ideas as to the source of your information and I think it only fair that at this point we give you an explanation of the kind of information with which we think we were working through Edgar Cayce.

Through the years we asked a great many questions about the source of Edgar Cayce's information. He explained it while in the trance state (he had no explanation while in his conscious state) by saying that in previous life experiences the soul entity had developed the ability to lay aside the physical consciousness and move in time and space. Thus in the period of a reading he could, through the subject given him, be in touch with the mind and body of an individual a thousand miles away and give, as he did thousands of times, accurate checkable descriptions of the physical condition of both the mind and the body of the individual. Frequently he described action in which this individual was involved taking place at the time of the reading. The Edgar Cayce records seemed to confirm the theory of survival of personality in a body form different from that we know in physical consciousness. He stressed the function of psychic perception through any or all of the five senses simultaneously. There were numerous references to communication with entities who had passed on but in no instance did he indicate a specific guide or control for any reading. Rather he described it as a movement of his own higher consciousness to contact the minds of entities on the earth plane and other planes of consciousness. He repeated what he saw, heard and felt. For example, we at no time had a change of voice or personality. Frequently it was as if he had interviewed an individual or simply had gone to a particular individual or place and picked up impressions. He worked in a state of unconsciousness, deep trance, or whatever you wish to call it.

We have been particularly interested in the information which you have gotten for us because, as I believe my brother mentioned to you in the beginning, it tended to confirm in several details the data which we secured through Edgar Cayce during experimental readings many years ago.

I have pointed out to my brother that it is quite possible that if information on the "site" coming from either Edgar Cayce or Mr. Gross is being picked up from the memory patterns of the personalities now existing of individuals involved in placing the cache that we are quite likely to have conflicting bits of information. Even conscious memory is notoriously bad and we are dealing with a physical area which has changed and is continuing to change constantly through the actual movement of large quantities of sand.

We must also consider the possibility that personalities on another plane of consciousness either do not desire that the cache be located or are simply having fun at our expense. Equally important are the co-existing theories that such entities are bound by their attachment to such caches and that a use of the monies for good purposes releases the individuals. Hence, we might well be doing a great many people a great service.

Without question, whatever be the source of our information, the ideals and purposes of the individuals involved are vitally important.

Frankly, we have been delighted and impressed with your frankness, directness and detachment.

I know that my brother is sending you some maps of the "site" and you can depend upon my full interest and cooperation. I look forward to the opportunity of meeting you at some later time.

Sincerely yours,
Hugh Lynn Cayce

At about the same time, I wrote to them also, though in a slightly different vein.

November 10, 1951

Dear Mr. Roberts and Mr. Gross:

It looks as if we are going to get nowhere with further photographs such as I have sent you. There are two other possibilities as I see it that may give better results:

1. I plan to make an accurate large scale map of the immediate area at White Hill. This map will show the top of hill, shoreline, areas where we have made excavations, and prominent landmarks as well as elevations of the various points. Along with this map I will enclose samples of the soil (on surface and as deep as we have dug) a piece of bark or wood or leaf from the oldest trees in immediate area, a piece of the Indian pottery, a sample of the bay water, and anything else that I think of that you might touch the rod to and try for a reaction on the map. This will take a while to prepare, but I will send it to you as soon as possible.

2. The other possibility, and of course the one I would like to see tried as I believe it to be the one most likely to be successful, is for you to come down to Virginia Beach and go over the hill in person. I realize you are busy with many other matters and that you hesitate to take time to go on what might be a wild goose chase. However, Virginia Beach isn't a bad place for a short vacation, especially in the summertime and it is only a few hours by plane from your home. Please do keep us in mind, and if time ever permits do consider coming down for what could be a relaxing vacation and would at least be a very interesting experiment.

I don't believe conclusions can be reached on any matter until every possibility and means of experiment has been tried, and I hope you will bear with us until some sort of conclusion is reached.

I appreciate your past cooperation and am open to any suggestions you may offer. I would be interested in your comments on Hugh Lynn's letter, any ideas on map and possible samples for reactions. I hope you will find it possible to stop by Virginia Beach in the near future.

Sincerely,
Edgar E. Cayce

On the 29th of November, my brother and I went to White Hill with a transit and tape, and setting up on the highest point of the hill, we made a detailed map of the area showing prominent trees, stumps, etc. We sent the map to our dowser along with a sample of sand from the hill, a piece of Indian pottery found there, a piece of bark from the big pignut hickory tree, a piece of a large pine stump at the water's edge, and a sample of water from the bay.

Mr. Gross's reply to our letter and samples seemed to justify our efforts. He returned the map with a number of notations. He spotted on the map another pignut hickory tree, several pine trees, and marked three locations where he got reactions to buried treasure. The first weekend we could get to the hill, we checked his latest results. We were elated. Exactly where he noted on the map we found a second small pignut hickory. Pine trees were found in the exact locations he noted, as was an old stump.

Our spirits were rejuvenated, for here was proof that Henry Gross was able to dowse accurately from a map. We considered another major effort of excavating. However, bad weather set in and for four months a combination of weather and personal business kept us from exploring further. In the spring of 1952, we received the following letter from Kenneth Roberts.

Dear Mr. Cayce:

When you're ready to resume work, and have your pump, hose and other things assembled on the site, you might send me a schedule of days when you are going to be working, and I'll do my best to send Henry Gross to Virginia Beach, so that you can take him out to your locations and let him do some pinpointing.

We'll do this for you at our own expense, as your reports have been far more thorough than most of those that are made by people for whom we try to do things. We have practically been driven out of working for private individuals, as they lack almost everything that would tend to further the work we're trying to do. That is to say, they lack courage, integrity, energy, money and sufficient intelligence to follow our instructions. The only way we can get any sort of adequate return is by working for corporations, and occasionally taking on individuals who are able to show their gratitude by putting their brains to work in a good cause.

Upon receipt of this long-awaited letter, the "treasure-hunting club" held a meeting and made plans for an all-out effort. It was arranged for Mr. Gross to come down on a Thursday, and that weekend we planned our assault on White Hill.

Hugh Lynn and I met Henry Gross as scheduled. We were both startled by his resemblence to our father in appearance and manner. At dinner we talked about his water dowsing feats and afterwards watched him demonstrate his technique with a dowsing rod. The rod appeared to actually twist in his hand with no conscious effort on his part. These demonstrations consisted of him "sensitizing" the dowsing rod by touching it to an object and then locating that object in a room. When he searched for underground water this "sensitizing" was unnecessary. We discussed his dowsing from maps as well as in the field and learned that he seemed to get a feeling of a "yes" or "no" answer when using the dowsing rod so that he could obtain answers to almost any question. The dowsing rod was surely either a stage prop or a catalyst for the expression of his particular psychic ability. Psychics or sensitives express their ability in many different ways and Hugh Lynn, particularly, was always eager to observe one in action. We were both spoiled, I suppose, by the scope of Edgar Cayce's ability and the accuracy of his "readings," and as a result, most psychics we encountered rated a poor second.

Friday, July 11, 1952—the day we had planned for months. The day dawned bright and clear and we shoved off in our heavily laden boat at 5:00 A.M. Upon arriving at White Hill, Mr. Gross set to work. He got reactions over two spots very near the places he had marked on the maps and photographs. Besides our high-speed pump we had a lower capacity pump and a quantity of flat sheet metal with which we constructed a sluiceway. By pumping water into this metal trough we had a means of carrying the sand away from where we dug. We had learned from experience that unless you used a tremendous quantity of water, the water-sand mix would sink into the sand after about 50 to 75 feet and you were kept busy keeping a channel open.

That day we worked like Trojans. We excavated the locations Mr. Gross indicated to almost the water level of the bay. Then we probed another 6 to 8 feet in the bottom of these holes with steel rods. The results were entirely negative—no gold, no silver, no jewels. We did hit a trace of ashes at about 11 feet at one location, and what looked like the remains of a rusty nail appeared in our sluiceway amidst the sand from about a 6-foot depth, but that was all.

It was a dejected crew that wearily cleaned up their equipment the next day and bid Henry Gross farewell. I am sure he was as disappointed as we were at the failure of our combined efforts.

What of the elusive treasure of White Hill? Did it ever really exist? Was it buried originally and later retrieved, or does it still lie undiscovered beneath the shifting sands? Was Edgar Cayce wrong when he gave the first reading about this cache? Did wrong attitudes, triggered by greed on the part of the parties requesting this reading, cause false or misleading information to be given? Why did Henry Gross get indications of a treasure both from maps and on location? Why was he right on water and on locating pine stumps and hickory trees from maps and completely wrong on a treasure location?

I doubt if I can answer these questions to everyone's satisfaction. Possibly information about the treasure was picked up by both Edgar Cayce and Mr. Gross from the minds of departed spirits of pirates or Indians who lived at the time the treasure was buried. Maybe the treasure *was* removed later. Maybe these spirits were having fun at our expense. Maybe physical changes in the hill and its vegetation cover left them as confused as we were as to its location in 1952. I don't know for sure. I do know that we investigated the southwest portion of White Hill where 20 to 25 feet straight down or in from the bay would bring one to water level. We moved tons of sand without any indication of Indian remains or buried loot. The fact that we never found any evidence of an Indian burying ground leads me to believe that we never dug in the right spot. However, the random auger holes never turned up any evidence of Indian remains, either. The only thing pertaining to Indians that we ever found was a quantity of broken pottery, and it was never found at any depth, but always near the surface of the hill, not more than a few inches under the sand.

Of course, our biggest drawback was that we didn't really know what we were looking for. Edgar Cayce never mentioned the size of the containers or their exact contents. We only supposed they contained enough gold and jewels to make them worth $1,000,000, Since papers were mentioned, maybe what is buried there is a map to a million-dollar treasure.

Would I ever go treasure-hunting there again? Well, if someone comes up with a metal locator with a 25- to 30-foot range on small objects, I would like to see it tried on the hill. Anything it detected could only be buried treasure, for the hill is surely pure sand. How about another psychic? Well, if he could prove he can locate buried metal objects, maybe; but to just go digging in the dark, I have done that. I will point out the hill to you on a map and show you the start of the trail there, but I'll take my sun on the golf course or at the beach. Oh yes, don't forget to take plenty of drinking water—there is none on the hill.

CHAPTER 9

Frustration At Kelly's Ford

Q-14. Describe the burying of the treasure at the time it was buried.

A-14. These are the conditions that existed when L. N. George, the paymaster, received the money in gold and silver. There was more than a washing tub full and preparations were being made to pay off the troops. They were in the tent on the side of the hill that rose from where the bridge used to cross over this river. The fires were all burning in preparation for the morning meal when they were attacked form the south by the Confederate forces. A hole was hurriedly dug by the side of those rocks in which the camp fire was burning nearest the paymaster's tent and the money was dumped in. Afterwards, George and those associated with him—one was first taken prisoner—were killed as they fled northward and to the east. [slightly paraphrased] . . . 3812–9, April 18, 1931

A whole washing tub full of gold and silver—enough to fire the imagination of any treasure-hunter!

This story properly begins on February 17, 1929. The same Mr. Prontes who two years later obtained the readings regarding the White Hill treasure wrote to Edgar Cayce from New York. His letter said, in part:

If you can send me the information concerning the location of the buried treasure near Washington, I believe that I can get sufficient money to make a good search for it. The buried treasure instrument that I was telling you about will be in New York this week and we will be able to use it for this purpose.

Evidently a reading had been given years before on a treasure buried near Washington, D. C. Just who obtained this reading and what information it contained may never be known, for it is missing from our files. As Edgar Cayce replied to Mr. Prontes:

Dear Mr. Prontes:

I don't know as I can even send you the information concerning the treasure buried near Washington. I will look it up and try to find it if possible, but you know it will be like looking for a needle in a haystack until we get our work correlated in such a way we will know how to put our fingers on it. That's why we need our data-statistician so very badly. We hope to get to work on this sometime in the near future, and then we will be able to answer a great many questions we can't right now.

I'm glad to report that our first patient (from the hospital established in Virginia Beach to check and follow suggestions from the readings) went home yesterday feeling the best, as he said, he ever did in his life, that he could remember. After the first couple of days he put on about a pound and a half each day—went home feeling fine.

Remember us to Mrs. Prontes and with kindest personal regards, I am,

Sincerely,

Edgar Cayce

Edgar Cayce couldn't find the information requested. The original reading had been removed from the files and never returned. On March 3, 1929, he gave a reading to recall this information.

Mrs. C: You will have before you the information given through these sources some years ago regarding the money lost by the Federal Troops near Washington, D.C. (Culpepper County, Va.) You will give us any information regarding this at the present time, as to how and where this may be located.

Mr. C: Near Brandywine Ford—yes, near Brandywine Ford. On the North banks of this Ford there is, and was, a large gulley that emptied into the Brandywine. In this region and this district were the troops of the Federal forces located when the Confederate forces came into the camp in the early morning of September 24, 1863, see? September 24, 1863. There was just a large washing tub full of twenty dollar gold pieces—now how many is that? These may be located in this hill as still lies between this large log here, just above the Ford and the gulley. It was buried, not deep, but has gotten much deeper in the years as they have passed. We are through. . . . 3812–1

While this reading confirms the general location of the buried gold, it is not very specific, but a copy of it was sent to Mr. Prontes. Edgar Cayce was busy giving physical readings and Mr. Prontes was moving around between New York, Washington, and Florida with all kinds of big schemes and deals cooking at once, so it was November 21, 1930, before he wrote again.

Dear Mr. Cayce:

If you have additional information on this treasure location as I notice in the reading that it says that information has been given before on this treasure —would appreciate it if you will forward same to me as quickly as possible as we may leave for Washington about Tuesday or Wednesday or next week.

Sincerely yours,
Mr. Prontes

Edgar Cayce wrote back what he remembered about the buried gold, and explained again that the original reading on this buried money was not in the files. At this time Mr. Prontes was in Ashland, Kentucky, preparing to go to Washington.

November 24, 1930

Dear Mr. Prontes:

Now, regarding the information about the location of the treasure near Washington—I think this was gotten some years ago for some people from Maryland, while we were in Birmingham, and they took that as their own— we have no copy of it. I'm sure you will find some record of this treasure in the war records, or of this amount being lost. This is the story as I remember it: There was some thirty or forty thousand dollars in silver sent to the Federal Army as a payroll. Just before it was paid out they were attacked by the Confederates, driven out of their position, and the money was buried by the quartermaster or paymaster department, and just where—or just how—seems to be the question. All of these seem to have either been captured, killed or lost in some way and the records lost as to the exact location of this. This is one, I think, of the several uncleared records of the government, and you may be able to obtain information in the war department about this. This happened, I think, in the year '62 or '63. This is as much as I can tell you of it.

I certainly hope that everything works out well for you. With kindest personal regards from all, I am

Sincerely,
Edgar Cayce

Mr. Prontes went to the Washington area, but was unable to find even the general location where the gold was supposed to be buried. On December 15, he wired Edgar Cayce:

DR. SMITH AND I HAVE BEEN MAKING DILIGENT SEARCH FOR PROPOSITION NEAR HERE WITHOUT SUCCESS STOP CAN YOU GIVE READING INDICATING NAME OF STATE. COUNTY, RIVER, AND FORD WHERE CACHED AND NAME OF NEAREST TOWN AND OTHER INFORMATION THAT WILL ASSIST STOP PLEASE WIRE OR PHONE COLLECT RALEIGH HOTEL REGARDS, PRONTES.

Cayce wired back: "ENGAGEMENT WAS SEPTEMBER 24, 1863 NEAR BRANDYWINE FORD."

Evidently Mr. Prontes was still unsuccessful in his search, and he and Dr. Smith returned to Virginia Beach for another reading, which was given December 20, 1930. They hoped to get specific instructions on how to locate the buried money.

Mrs. C: You will have before you the bodies and the enquiring minds of Mr. Prontes and Dr. Smith, present in this room, seeking information as to name of state and county, and more definite description of location of buried treasure at or near Brandywine Ford. The information will be given in such a manner as will be understood by the above parties.

Mr. C: Yes, we have bodies, the enquiring minds, Mr. Prontes and Dr. Smith, present in this room; also those conditions and circumstances as surround treasure sought. These—and different phases we have had before.

The information as has been given, the information given more recently to each—and separately—has indicated the place and manner in which this may be sought out. This should be done at a time when the moon is new, and just after this has set. On the third or sixth day, then, of the new moon, seek same.

The roads have changed somewhat, and on the southwest side—or farther from the location—but the logs are very close to same. Seek out same with the instruments that have been devised for those of seeking *silver,* for this will be found in greater quantities, see? Ready for questions.

Q-1. Is what is now Kelly's Ford the same that was at that time known as Brandywine Ford?

A-1. The same.

Q-2. Then were the above parties on the right location Wednesday afternoon, December 17th, 1930?

A-2. Very near, and almost over same.

Q-3. There was information given Mr. Prontes and Dr. Smith through a medium that a blue light would guide them at dusk and stop over the treasure. Is this correct?

A-3. Correct. There is an emanation from every character of metal, and may be seen under varied or different circumstances. Those of gold produce a glow between that of orange and purple, or purple tinged with orange. Silver and its alloy produce that of a dull gray-blue, with a white, or those of the whitish hue. These are those sought in the present, and may be found at time given. The ones *placing* same there at the time are *also* aiding in its being located. The paymaster, or quartermaster's department, headed by that of Captain Capps at the time.

Q-4. Who is giving this information at this time?

A-4. Capps and Snyder.

Q-5. Was the boulder that Mr. Prontes moved on December 17th near the location?

A-5. This almost an equal distance between boulder and the double logs as are near there, see?

Q-6. Is the direction north, south, east or west from that boulder?

A-6. Better that the instrument be used in locating, going over this proposition or position, or area between this and the log, for in this area will the location be made. Some scattered, but there was more than a tub full when put there!

Q-7. Have they the location of the gulley right?

A-7. That's near right.

Q-8. What is the name of the instrument that should be used in locating this?

A-8. The silver divining rod.

Q-9. Where will they obtain one?

A–9. There are many of these. Some are not so strong as others—but seek something for self, at least!

Q–10. Any other information that would be of help at this time, that may be given?

A–10. Now the lights, as given, will be seen on the third or the sixth day the better, and will be seen when things are the quietest or when there is the least stir, see? and will be as emanations from the earth itself in this area. Then place rod or instrument in this spot, and then dig it up! because it isn't very deep! We are through for the present. . . . 3812–2

Rather a strange reading. Note that Mr. Prontes and Dr. Smith had located the general area of the ford and former camp site and had been standing almost over the buried gold and silver. They had also been getting advice from another psychic or medium and they were advised to use their own abilities to locate the buried money.

Notice how important it is to phrase questions properly. For example, consider the third question: "There was information given Mr. Prontes and Dr. Smith through a medium that a blue light would guide them at dusk and stop over the treasure. Is this correct?" What is the question here? Is Mr. Prontes asking Edgar Cayce whether a medium made such a statement or is he asking whether the statement made by the medium was true? It might be interpreted either way. Often the reason that ambigious answers were obtained in readings is that ambigious questions were asked.

Some psychics or sensitives claim to see an aura around living individuals that may indicate the person's physical condition and/or emotional state. This reading states that some sensitives are also able to see an emanation or radiation from metals such as gold and silver. It advised Mr. Prontes and Dr. Smith to search in this manner, even suggesting a specific time of the month and night. It also suggested the use of a divining rod or dowsing rod, another device used by some psychics to locate objects, generally underground water. In my opinion a dowsing rod is merely a stage prop, a means used by a psychic or sensitive to manifest his ability. In many regards, Edgar Cayce suggested that individuals could develop their own innate psychic ability, and he advised them to do so.

Notice that the answer to the fourth question states that Edgar Cayce received some of this information by his subconscious mind contacting the minds of departed Union soldiers, a Captain Capps and someone named Snyder. This raises more questions than it answers because there is no evidence that this Capps or Snyder knew any more about the location of the treasure than the ones seeking it. The question of when they are describing it also arises, since there had been many changes due to flooding of the river, growth of trees, etc., that somewhat changed the appearance of the terrain. It is doubtful if the ones who hid the money in 1863 would recognize the old camp site were they able to see it almost 100 years later.

Four days later Edgar Cayce gave another reading. Mr. Prontes had been unable to see any emanation, radiation, or lights from the buried money, though they had dug a hole in the general area where they thought the money might be buried. Notice particularly the suggestion given Edgar Cayce for this next reading and his answer to the question of why they did not see any radiating lights or locate the treasure:

Mrs. C: You will have before you the information given through these sources on December 20, 1930, regarding the buried treasure near what is now Kelly's Ford, and also the recent efforts of Dr. Smith and Mr. Prontes to locate this treasure. You will explain why they did not see the light, and give explicit instructions as to which direction and the exact distance the treasure is from the hole which they dug in that vicinity last.

Mr. C: Yes, we have the information as has been given respecting treasure. This, as we find, *has not been followed* in a manner in keeping with the instructions as were given as to how, when, where, they would see, know *and* locate same. Is the purpose, then, in keeping with that as outlined, *or are their motives of self's own making,* and is it to be found as they would seek, or as they are directed? Would the finding of same bring those conditions that are understandable to the experiences of the individuals, or do they only give or lend *to* them that which may be used as a stumbling stone to themselves? These they should answer within themselves. Will those instructions as were *given* be followed in the manner outlined, the lights or emanations as has been given that come from such *may* be seen. Are they to be seen whenever desired, or are they to be seen when there are conditions as are known in a material plane as cause and effect? or are they to set the cause and the effect also? There are emanations from the combinations as outlined.

The location as dug is not so close to the place where same will be found. Best, then, as would be given in the present, to take this as the starting point. Secure those indicators as outlined. Be patient, and be particular that that as has been given must be done in the manner outlined. This, as we find, will be found north by northwest from this spot. Follow those instructions. We are through for the present. . . . 3812–3

Notice how Mr. Prontes and Dr. Smith were berated for not following instructions and that their motives were questioned. Yet the reading was patiently aimed at helping them even though they wanted to search in their own way instead of following instructions.

I will always wonder what would have happened if they had followed Edgar Cayce's instructions. Suppose they had gone to the location on the third or sixth day of the new moon, just after it had set, when things were quiet. Would they have seen a ghostly glow emanating from the very spot where the treasure lay? Would this have saved them hours of useless digging? Could one seek in this manner now?

Meanwhile another party and his two cousins had become interested in trying to locate this treasure and had been working with Mr. Prontes and Dr. Smith. Early in January 1931, this new group obtained a reading. They were trying to hold an unselfiish attitude toward the undertaking so that better information might be obtained through Edgar Cayce. This is not an easy reading to understand and I am sure it was not understood then. I have italicized what I think are important statements, which if understood then, would have saved everyone concerned many hours of useless labor. Note that Mr. Prontes's motives were specifically condemned. There was a definite statement that the time was not right and an intimation that the undertaking of these people to find this treasure at this time would be unsuccessful.

Mrs. C: You will have before you the bodies and the enquiring minds of Edgar Cayce, Mr. A, Mr. B and Mr. C, present in this room. You will also have the proposition which has been in mind of each for the past few days as follows: It is the desire of these four to aid mankind through the carrying out of the work of Edgar Cayce in absolute accordance with information obtained through his readings. These four pledge themselves to carry out in detail and in accord with the ideal of this group to help mankind, any advice and information which may be obtained through these forces that lead to the finding of buried treasures. One half of each treasure so found will be set aside as a fund to be administered by the four as directed through these readings to build hospitals, schools, carry on social service work and generally aid man to help himself. The rest will be equally divided among the four who will then contribute from their share the necessary amounts for the next expedition. It is the desire that this work expand and grow to become a great force for good in the world. Please give us advice and guidance as to the practicability and feasibility of this plan and if it is in accord with the will of the Creative Forces, guide us in the initial steps for this work. Please answer the questions regarding this which we will ask you.

Mr. C: Yes, we have the bodies, the enquiring minds, Edgar Cayce, Mr. A, Mr. B, and Mr. C, present in this room. Also the ideas and the ideals of each as concerning the information as may be given as respecting beneficial effects as may be obtained from same, in aiding mankind through the various channels. Also that manner in which these seek at this time to obtain such financial assistance and aid, and the distribution of such.

In considering such an undertaking, there are many conditions, many things, to be considered pro and con. There are many conditions already existent in the affairs of each, as well as in relations to others. *As has been given, these should be rather a unity of thought* than of individuals' attempts to take the varied phases of same and work from individual channels.

In the present situations, we find the idea and ideal of those who are particularly concerned at this time is plausible, feasible, and a workable situation; *yet the time for same is not the proper period, either in the development of the ideal in the minds of either of those concerned, or in the affairs as they exist in the present situation,* for, as has oft been given, "Let not thine good be *evil* spoken of." *In the present situation we would find misunderstandings arising from the efforts,* whether they be successful or only partially so, or an entire failure.

Then, the question naturally arises in the minds of these present, as to the manner in which each would conduct themselves to better prepare themselves, to collaborate their efforts as a group, in a manner that *will* be acceptable, understandable, and *meet* the situations in the lives of each, concerning their desire to aid, to use their efforts as a stimuli to mankind's development in the affairs of individuals, in the affairs of groups, masses, nations. *These apparently have been rejected in many ways by those apparently in charge, or in active association with the affairs of that being attempted.*

The discovery of treasures, that have been placed—or misplaced—has oft been given as a channel through which a service may—*at its proper time*—come, for the development, of the Edgar Cayce phenomena—this should not be a means to an end, but an end to a means to carry on; and, later as each —prepare themselves, there will be given what each *is* to do, to accomplish more for themselves and for mankind. . . . 3812-4

As I said, this is not an easy reading to read or to understand, and it is quoted for the benefit of those who want to understand why psychic information sometimes seems inaccurate or misleading. For this particular group it was excellent advice, beautifully stated; but the advice was ignored. It certainly sounds as if these readings were saying that it would be best for all concerned if this treasure *were not* discovered then. It was as if Edgar Cayce could look into the probable future and see trouble, quarreling, and unhappiness among the members of the group if the treasure were found.

In spite of the clearcut warnings that this was not the time for the undertaking, the group continued their search. There then occurred an interesting event. One of the members of the group had a dream in which he discovered an iron tub filled with manuscripts and a few pieces of gold. He heard a voice saying, "This is a small amount which if used rightly will lead to finding the great fortune." The group was encouraged by this dream and sought an interpretation of it in a reading. However, the reading reiterated that it meant the treasure would not be discovered until the proper time: "This, as is seen, is an individual experience of the entity, as a test—for the greater portion of same is true, yet *would not, could not* be located until the proper time, the proper attitude, the proper conditions were within the experiences of each individual. . . . 3812-5."

In answer to a direct question for specific suggestions the answer was: "A-4. These have been set in *very definite* lines. Use that thou hast! Do all you know to do at present, as it were. *Don't try to hasten that thou knowest is not the best! . . .* 3812-5."

Meanwhile, Mr. Prontes was jumping between Washington, New York, and Florida with his fingers in a dozen different pies. Bad weather and "big deals" prevented Mr. Prontes from further explorations at Kelly's Ford until April 1931. By then he had secured some sort of electrical device that he tried to use to locate the treasure. There is no record as to what sort of device it was, but evidently it was crude and ineffective.

On April 16 another reading was requested. (I am sure that sometimes Edgar Cayce felt that these readings on buried treasure were a waste of time, time that could have been used to cure a score of sick.)

Mrs C: You will have before you the treasure buried near what is now Kelly's Ford, Culpepper County, Virginia, and the work done yesterday, April 15, 1931, by Mr. Prontes, Dr. Smith and son, Mr. A and Mr. B, attempting to locate this treasure. Please give them advice in a way and manner that will be understandable, considering the property as it now lies, as to how to proceed to locate this treasure. You will answer the questions which they will ask.

Mr. C: Yes, we have the operations that have been made in search for treasure at Kelly's Ford—

As, we find, in the second location as was made—*this has been excavated to the west and the south from where the treasure, or greater portion, will be found*—where there are indications of burned wood, ashes, and the like. Will there be the checking of this location with the vibrating machine, it will outline for them the location where this may be found—see? Ready for questions.

Q-1. How deep is the treasure from top of the ground in its present condition?

A-1. From three to three and a half feet.

Q-2. How many feet from present—

A-2. Locate same with machine, rather than trying to measure from here —because it's scattered about—where the ashes were.

Q-3. Have we been using the instrument correctly? If not, how should it be used?

A-3. Make same for the depths that do not extend so deep—see? In other respects, very good—but atmospheric conditions have interfered, though the atmosphere, time and period show for indications from emanations—as has been seen. This, while not in the exact spot, is where they should use instrument for locating—see?

Q-4. What is indicated by the instrument in the second location on top of the small mound not yet dug into?

A-4. This where there will be found portions of that which will be very interesting.

Q-5. Was the gray light we saw near the first hole dug an indication of the location of the treasure?

A-5. Indicator of those emanations, as has been described, from treasure buried.

Q-6. Any other advice to these?

A-6. Follow these as we have given—see? We are through for the present.

The first paragraph of this reading tells them they are digging in the wrong place; they were *south* and *west* of the buried money. There is some question as to how Edgar Cayce interpreted the word "present" in answering Question 1. Was he "seeing" the money as it was in 1863 or 1931? Remember Capps and Snyder; were they giving the directions? Also, there is a statement that one or more of the party saw a gray light.

Two days later, presumably after some hard digging, another reading was taken and a number of questions were asked and answered, some answers tinged with a wry sense of humor. Notice that the first paragraph answers the suggestion directly, saying the reason they haven't found the treasure is that they haven't dug in the right place!

Mrs. C: You will have before you the region known as Kelly's Ford in Culpepper Co., Va., the treasure which is buried there and the work done in attempting to locate this treasure by Mr. Prontes, Dr. Smith, Mr. A and Mr. B. Please direct them as to the next definite steps to take in locating this treasure, giving the reasons for the failure so far. You will answer the questions which will be asked regarding same.

Mr. C: Yes, we have the location, the operations, the individuals. In the region—as has been indicated by the operations—as we find, the reason, *they haven't dug in the right place!* While these have extended in a part over the areas as has been indicated, both by the information and by the indicator. Where the light shone, and in the area where the pit—as was in the placing of same in the logs, or between the logs—trees have grown in the present, and this naturally has altered the grounds, and the changes—but just keep on working there—we would find we would locate it—there's no cause from individuals or those that prevent same from other sources, but we would keep the operations until the locations were made. Follow with each day's operations those indications with the indicator, and follow those until they are exposed—all those metals and conditions that caused the vibrations to be altered, see? [*Note:* This was an old battleground. Sounds like extraneous material such as bullets, pieces of metal equipment, etc., may have interfered with the metal locator's functioning.]

As we find, the indications will be best found when those of the logs and stones that covered—and about the moneys themselves, see—are exposed. Go *into* them! Loose, burned stones—where fires were builded against same, and while these are in part pushed asunder, they still show the indications of fire on same.

Q-1. Is the hole in which we have found traces of ashes, broken dishes—

A-1. Follow the ashes, on that level—see? These extend towards the tree. They also extend towards the *wall*—see?

Q-2. Should we go toward the wall or toward the tree?

A-2. Go both, if it's indicated by the indicator!

Q-3. Have we gone deep enough with this excavation?

A-3. In parts. Some of it is too deep—wasn't necessary, but we will find that we will follow these to that as has been given—just given, see?

Q-4. In what direction should we proceed to dig into the location of the treasure, and can this be done best by digging in from the present hole or starting another hole?

A-4. Follow the line of the ashes! Can that be just by starting another, or continuing in the one that's there?

Q-5. We have estimated that this region has filled in about three feet with the soft dirt since the time the treasure was placed there? Is this correct and how deep in the—

A-5. It's six and a half feet, you see, in the depth from the top—though in many places it will be found to fill more than this—see?

Q-6. Is the bottom of the present hole over the treasure? and if so, how deep must we go to reach it?

A-6. Follow the ashes! Where they dip, dip! following the indicator in each day's operations—see? or half day's operation would be better.

Q-7. Is the treasure located more to the East toward the top of the mound or to the North toward the side of the mound?

A-7. To the side of the mound. Follow that as indicated by the indicator and by the ash. Be found to run both ways, or it turns as it comes in, as we find it.

Q-8. Is it near any of the rocks which formed the mound or the foundation for the N.E. end of the old bridge?

A-8. As is indicated, it's *behind* some rocks, see? those that are burned.

Q-9. Is it behind the burned rocks that we have uncovered?

A-9. You haven't uncovered 'em yet, that have it—or you would have recovered it if you had!

Q-10. Was the excavation on top of the hill made in the right place? Should we go deeper or more in which direction and how deep from the top of the present surface?

A-10. Following the ash, on the level where it is indicated.

Q-11. Haven't located any ashes on top of the hill.

A-11. Then dig in until you find them!

Q-12. Should we go deeper?

A-12. Follow the indicator.

Q-13. Are they using the indicator correctly?

A-13. Using correctly.

Q-14. Please describe the burying of the treasure at the time it was buried. . . . 3812-9

The answer to Q-14 was given at the beginning of this story.

The questions and answers in this reading border on the ludicrous. It could be the conversation between an impatient parent and an argumentative child. At the time I suppose the group was trying to get specific information, but upon looking back on the reading the questions seem inane, and it is a wonder Cayce was so patient.

Work at Kelly's Ford continued into May. Reading 3812-11, taken May 1, 1931, indicated a misapplication of the information given, possible misuse of the indicator or metal locator they were using, and cross-purposes among members of the digging party. This reading insisted the money was intact and still there.

Mrs. C: You will have before you the treasure located near Kelly's Ford, Culpepper Co., Va., and the work which has been done in attempting to locate this by Mr. Prontes, Dr. Smith and son, Mr. A, Mr. B and Mr. C, especially that work done on April 29, 1931, in accordance with information received through these sources. Please tell us if we followed this information correctly, or what mistakes were made that prevented us from locating this treasure. Please direct us as to how to proceed to locate this treasure now. Please explain our failures so we may understand it.

Mr. C: Yes, we have the treasure as has been located in Culpepper County, Virginia, near Kelly's Ford. Also those operations, those searches as made with the information, with individuals, and the failures so far in locating same.

As has been given, we find the treasure still intact, and that in all apparent manners and ways the information as given has been followed in accordance with instructions through these sources, even to checking same, sinking shaft, and such.

In considering, then, these conditions, apparently there is fault in some respects. As has been given, *many* conditions enter in, in seeking for such sources of that that becomes powers in the use of same, especially in seeking same through such sources, such channels; *yet when each are in accord,* and the *purposes,* the *desires,* the *aims* are ONE, and they in accord with that as is set as purposes and aims, then apparently there should be that complete success; yet each have *not* examined themselves. This does not alter the conditions as to whether the treasure is here or there, or as to whether there has been a mis-application of the information given.

Then, in seeking same—and in the manner as to how each should act or conduct their *own* lives as to make the complete success of this undertaking:

The manners, the ways, have been set before each as to how they shall conduct their activities. *That* an individual application.

Then, in the circumstances, in the conditions as exist, how shall these individuals, as individuals—and as a group—proceed to locate that being sought?

So long as the indicator and the information is in accord, so long *seek* in *that* place *indicated* in the information and by the indicator. As to how this shall be done—these, perforce, must needs be done to *meet* the *physical existent* conditions as exist in the *immediate* place and *immediate* surroundings. As to how, these are here. As to the manner each individual is to conduct self, that with the individual. Because rocks, that apparently are of an origin that would indicate that these could *not* have been placed there since the placing of the cache—Is the information in the same source of reasoning as is the growing of nature itself? Is there any more unreasonableness that this may have *grown* into place, than that even the *place* could *be* pointed out either by forces not understood in natural means or forces not understood in the realm of mind or mental things? Then, act in accord with that as *seemeth* best unto each individual *as* a group; for, as we find, the moneys—as given —are intact. Ready for questions.

Q-1. Is the treasure located directly under the blue rock which we struck in the bottom of present excavation?

A-1. As indicated, as given—so long as the indicator *and* the information point to one and the same, then seek there.

Q-2. How thick is this rock?

A-2. No matter how thick, if it's to be searched through—then seek!

Q-3. How far does it extend to the West?

A-3. Over the whole ledge.

Q-4. Is the depth down to the rock struck in the bottom of the excavation the correct depth?

A-4. If it was, the treasure would have been uncovered if it was wholly so—would it not? Let's be consistent and reasonable with those things that are to be reasoned from the material viewpoint. Let's understand that forces in nature, forces in man, forces in the soul of man, sources as are in the realm of man's undertakings, are being used. Use each in *their* respective sphere. We are through. . . . 3812-11

In the opening paragraphs Edgar Cayce said the treasure was intact and that, although it seemed that the suggestions given were being followed, apparently something or someone was at fault. He then stated that many factors must be considered when information is sought from a psychic source: Evidently complications arose because more than one person was seeking information. If the group effort was to be a success, all the parties involved had to be in accord with one another. Their purposes, desires, and aims must not be self-centered but directed toward what each had agreed to do when the undertaking was organized. There is a flat statement that each person has not examined his own motives and an intimation that all are not in harmony. He also said that in approaching the hunt from a material angle, natural laws cannot be flaunted. He stressed that the search should be conducted where the metal locator and the information given in the reading agreed. A good example is given in the next few paragraphs of the reading. Evidently bedrock had been encountered. This was not a few loose stones but a large ledge of solid rock. Here Cayce stated that it is unreasonable to expect that sort of rock to have grown in that place over the treasure; obviously this could not be the correct location, or the treasure would have been located before this bedrock was hit. He admonished the seekers to try to understand "the forces in nature, forces in man, forces in the soul of man" and to "use each in their respective sphere."

It sounds to me as if Edgar Cayce was trying to tell these people something about the laws regarding the accuracy of psychic information. He insisted that the motives or attitudes of the parties involved were important in setting up a sort of empathy between the seekers and the psychic that directed his subconscious toward the proper source of the information. Where greed, avarice, and selfishness centered in these factors seemed to misdirect Edgar Cayce's subconscious mind so that the source he contacted was of like character. Thus, instead of getting positive accurate direction, the information was muddled and colored by the sources from which it was received, sources that may not even have had accurate information about the hidden treasure.

Another reading on May 12, 1931, gave personal advice to the parties concerned and suggested searching where the electrical locator and the information given in the readings were in accord. Digging was continued and a sizable hole was made. It was no longer possible to throw shovelfuls of dirt out of the hole. The clay had to be hauled out in buckets. When it rained, water collected in the hole and had to be bailed out by hand. No pumps or any kind of mechanical equipment were used.

Additional readings were given and digging continued into the summer. All sorts of evidence of a battle were uncovered—buttons, bullets, pieces of metal, even some logs, rocks, and ashes. All felt they were very close but they kept having trouble getting any reliable indication with their metal locator. I have serious doubts about the accuracy of such a device in 1931, and am convinced that none of the treasure-hunters knew how to operate it properly. This fact is clearly indicated in an answer to a question in another reading:

Q-3. Is the instrument being used working correctly?
A-3. Hasn't been used, or hasn't worked correctly, as yet! . . . 3812-18

Reading 3812-17 repeated what had been given earlier, that they had not dug in the right place, but should dig north and east towards an old abutment. (Note that reading 3812-8 said they were south and west of the location of the cache.) Obviously, they should have dug toward the north and east. Somehow they had trouble following instructions.

The last reading on Kelly's Ford was given on July 10, 1931. Suggestion:

You will give specific directions for recovering this treasure, using such markers as are now visible as points from which to work, and you will answer the questions I will ask.

Mr. C: Yes, we have the operations here, as have been made in attempting to recover the treasure here, near Kelly's Ford, Culpepper County, Virginia.

Under existing physical conditions in the present, *little may be accomplished very soon.*

In the operations, as has been given, there should be made the check with the instrument and with information given. When these do not check, then cease operations until there is that understanding in the mind of each that are seeking same as to what, how, what for, and the conditions that have been set by each that have been seeking; *for that as has been promised must be fulfilled, every whit.* This is not just a material circumstance with which these operating are dealing, for they have promised much to self as well as to the Forces, or Sources, from which information has been or may come. Then, when there is cross feelings, or cross connections, there may be expected those things that will bring about destructive forces; for, as we find, the treasure is there, and they are very near to same—it being closer, or toward the abutment. *We do not find that they would locate, until they have made themselves right, that each may obtain or know within themselves that, that being sought*

is in accord with that which has been promised, as well as that they do.
. . . 3812-18

In spite of the professed good intentions of the members of the treasure-hunting expedition, there must have been doubts, fears, and cross-purposes among them. They must have become discouraged when water began seeping into the hole from the river. They were discouraged at finding logs and ashes but no money. I heard later that Mr. Prontes had procured a pistol and some burlap bags and that when the treasure was discovered he planned to take control of it for himself—a fine example of the diverse attitudes of the party!

After this last reading the hopes of finding anything were extinguished and the project was abandoned.

Is the gold and silver still there, scattered among the logs and ashes of a long-forgotten campfire? Edgar Cayce insisted it was there in 1931. Could modern metal detectors and earth-moving equipment locate this cache? Certainly well-equipped treasure-hunters today would have a better chance than that petulant party with no mechanical equipment and no reliable metal locator. If you could find the general location of the gulley that emptied into the Brandywine near the old bridge abutment at what was known as Kelly's Ford, you might shave off the ground with a bulldozer a foot at a time checking the area with a metal locator. When you came to rocks, logs, and ashes you might look more carefully. But in an area like that there were a lot of campfires. Be sure you dig into the right one.

CHAPTER 10

The Lost Dutchman Mine

So many tales have been written about the Lost Dutchman mine that it is beyond the scope of this book to repeat them all here. Briefly the story is this:

In about 1848 a Spanish prospector, Don Miguel Peralta, discovered an extremely rich vein of gold in the Superstition Mountains of Arizona near Weaver's Needle. With a party of miners he worked the vein and was doing very well until they were attacked by the Apaches. In a short and bloody encounter the miners were wiped out. The secret of the mine's location died with the miners, and for nine years it remained lost. Then in 1857 a wandering desert prospector named Jacob Walz stumbled onto the mine. Walz was close-mouthed, suspicious, and friendless. He worked alone and never filed a claim, for to do so would have disclosed the mine's location. Such ore specimens as he infrequently showed were reputed to be of extremely rich quality. Walz died in 1891 without ever revealing his secret.

Since Walz's death hundreds of men have scoured the area seeking the mine, the "Lost Dutchman." Legends and superstitions grew as fast as the seekers. There are 18 recorded deaths in the hunt for gold in the Superstition Mountains, but students of the legends say the number should be nearer 200, for many who wandered into the Superstition Mountains were never heard from again. Why hasn't the mine been located? The answer to this question has intrigued students of the Arizona desert for years. Some believe the earthquake of 1887 may have destroyed the mine or the landmarks.

These stories interested one man who requested a reading on the mine. The suggestion and reading are as follows:

Mrs. C: You will have before you Mr. X present in this room, and his enquiring mind, together with the gold mine discovered by Pedro Peralta and later worked by Jacob Walz known as "The Dutchman," in Pinal County, in the central portion of the State of Arizona. There you will find a high peak known as "La Sombrera" or "Weaver's Needle." In Needle Canyon, a canyon running north from the base of the peak, you will find a large Saquaro cactus, marked, or that has been marked by four stones stuck into the trunk. From this marker, you will tell us exactly how far, and in which direction to go to find the gold mine now known as "The Dutchman," describing in detail all landmarks from this marker leading directly to the mine. You will then answer the questions, as I ask them:

Mr. C: Yes, we have the enquiring mind, Mr. X, present in this room; and those conditions that exist as legends and those as realities pertaining to the lost mine or Dutchman Mine.

In undertaking directions for locations of this from the present conditions, many things should be taken into consideration—as to whether descriptions would apply to those periods when this was put in the way of being hidden and/or those that would apply to the present day surroundings.

For time in its essence—while it is one, in space there has been made a great variation by the activities of the elements and the characters that have been in these areas.

For these are held as sacred grounds by groups who have, from period to period, changed the very face of the earth or the surroundings, for the very purpose of being misleading to those who might attempt to discover or to desecrate (to certain groups) those lands.

As we find, if we would locate this—from the present outlook:

We would go from the cactus marked here, in the Canyon, some 5, 10, 20, 30, 37½ yards to the north by west—north by west—to a place where, on the side of the hills, there is a white rock—almost pure white—almost as a triangle on top.

Turn from here—for you can't get over some of the ground going directly to the east—turn almost directly to the east, and just where there is the crossing of the deep gulch, we will find the entrance to the Dutch Mine. This has been covered over, though to begin at the lower portion of the gulch we would find only about 6 feet before we would reach pay dirt in gold. Ready for questions.

Q-1. How rich is this vein?

A-1. It's rich enough to work. About, at the present rate, five to six thousand dollars a ton.

Q-2. Describe the type of ore.

A-2. Impregnations with loose gold.

Q-3. Is it covered over? If so, by what?

A-3. Rock, very much like the surrounding country.

Q-4. How deep is it from the surface?

A-4. If from the surface, about eight to ten feet. If you want to get to it, commence at the lower edge of the Canyon and work under it— towards the east, see?

Q-5. Give instructions for placing monuments and filing claim?

A-5. That must be done from the material angle. Just so there's taken in enough to include all this area for about a thousand yards each way.

Q-6. Give any further information about other mines in this group which may be helpful.

A-6. We would give plenty of them here—the silver mine in the Lost Sheep, which is over the hill on the other side towards the border, you see, that's the most valuable mine in Arizona. We are through for the present.

As far as is known, Mr. X never followed these directions, or if he did, he never located the Lost Dutchman. Is that cactus still standing with the four stones in its trunk? Is the white triangular rock still visible above the gulch? Want to trek into the superstitions? Or would you rather try to find the Lost Sheep mine, the most valuable mine in Arizona?

Before you set out, remember what Edgar Cayce said in the opening of this last reading, ". . . many things should be taken into consideration," whether the descriptions apply to the time the mine was being worked or the present time. This last reading would seem to indicate that the description was being given from the present. However, no mention was made concerning the source of the information. Who in the "present" knew where the mine was? No one! Was Edgar Cayce seeing it clairvoyantly? If so, why couldn't the man for whom the reading was given follow the directions and find it? Is it possible that the mine is there and he simply never looked in the right place?

CHAPTER 11

Oil Wells

October 12, 1920

FLUSH PRODUCTION DESDEMONA LUCKY BOY NUMBER TWO
BETTER THAN SIX HUNDRED BARRELS, FIRST DRILLED
THIRTY-FIVE HUNDRED FEET AND CONSIDERED DRY, CAYCE
ADVISED PLUG AROUND THREE THOUSAND, SHOOT AND
WOULD PRODUCE OIL, THIS DONE. SHOT AT TWENTY-NINE
HUNDRED EIGHTY. PRODUCTION. SOME CONSIDERED CAYCE
A WONDER. LETTER FOLLOWS.

JOS. B. LONG
VICE PRESIDENT
HOME NATIONAL BANK
CLEBURNE, TEXAS

The reading described in this telegram started Edgar Cayce, a
Selma, Alabama, photographer, on a bizarre series of experiences that
almost destroyed his psychic ability.

When Dad gave this reading (which has been lost), he had never
been in Texas. So far as can be ascertained, he had absolutely no
knowledge of oil wells in general, much less of the Lucky Boy #2,
which was described to him as a dry hole. Within the next three years,
Edgar Cayce and his friend, David E. Kahn, whom he involved in the
undertaking, traveled thousands of miles by automobile and train
raising money, getting oil leases, giving readings, and talking with

people throughout Texas, Kentucky, Georgia, Pennsylvania, New York, and Ohio. In these years, they saw thousands of dollars spent, strings of tools lost in wells, leases run out, and friends turned to enemies. But they saw also gas and oil appear at levels the reading indicated, people respond to the help received through the physical readings, and a personal friendship grow strong between an ex-Army captain and a Selma photographer that was to enrich and change both their lives (see *My Life with Edgar Cayce* by David E. Kahn as told to Will Oursler).

Edgar Cayce went west to meet the people who had put money into Desdemona Lucky Boy #2. He asked Kahn, who was just returned from overseas, to join him to take the readings. Information was first given on the Sam David oil well at Comyn, Texas. Its story is partly told in the following letter from M. C. Sanders, a driller and investor. This well never produced, and some of those associated with it believed that it was sabotaged. Edgar Cayce and Dave Kahn almost got shot on the site of the well, but I am getting ahead of my story.

1/22/21   Affidavit: M. C. Sanders   3777-1

THE STATE OF TEXAS
COUNTY OF JOHNSON

This is to certify that I have known Mr. Edgar Cayce for some years.

Having been connected with the Sam Davis Oil Company, directly looking after the drilling of their well No. One with which we had been having considerable trouble, also the said well having practically been abandoned by the original drillers, some of the stockholders believing production could be had out of this well, I decided to secure a reading from Mr. Edgar Cayce as to the well. He gave us this reading, instructing us to proceed with the well, we putting it in the proper condition. He also informed us that we would get oil, and that as we progressed at certain depths we would get showings of oil and gas and finally make out of this well a paying producer.

We followed Mr. Cayce's advice and were successful in freeing the well of obstructions which it contained, the result of an inexperienced, previous driller. Also, we found *that the oil and gas showed up in this well identically at the depths that Mr. Cayce had predicted. We also found these obstructions at the various depths predicted by Mr. Cayce.* We were also successful in freeing this well of these obstructions and getting same in good condition, all of which was through the reading that Mr. Cayce had given us.

We find this well, at the present time, in splendid condition, showing every sign of a good producer, just as Mr. Cayce indicated. However, I will say that we have not, as yet, finished same; but fully believe that same will prove a good producer when we have proceeded to the depth Mr. Cayce advised us to go, which is around about one hundred feet more. Without a doubt, I consider Mr. Cayce a wonderful man and have implicit confidence in his powers.

Witness my hand this the 22nd day of January 1921.

/s/ M. C. Sanders

Sworn and subscribed to before me this the 22nd day of January, 1921.

/s/ M. P. Allard
Notary Public, Johnson County, Texas.

While the Sam Davis well was still uncertain, Cayce and Kahn, in good faith, raised money to set up the Cayce Petroleum Company, which then leased various properties on which Cayce indicated in readings there was oil. My father was looking for the funds to build a hospital, and Kahn wanted to help him and make a million on the side. Money for the operations was secured on the strength of letters like this one from Mr. Long who was vice president of a Cleburne, Texas, bank.

1/22/21   Affidavit: Jos. B. Long: 3777–2

THE STATE OF TEXAS
COUNTY OF JOHNSON

M. P. Allard, Notary Public, Johnson County Personally appeared before me, this 22nd day of January, 1921, Mr. Joseph B. Long, known to me, who says:

This is to certify that I have known Mr. Edgar Cayce for the past three years, and have witnessed some of his readings in connection with business matters, and I consider him possessed with wonderful powers which are not easily understood.

I witnessed a reading he gave on the Lucky Boy Oil Company's property situated near Desdemona, Texas, and *said reading was, in all things, correct.* Mr. Cayce, at the time, had not seen this property and had no personal knowledge of its affairs.

Mr. Cayce has also given me readings on some business matters which have proven absolutely true and which were helpful to me in a very material way in my business pursuits. I consider Mr. Cayce a most wonderful man possessed of marvelous powers. He is also a conscientious, christian gentleman, and to my certain knowledge has refrained from using his powers for exhibition purposes, to my certain knowledge having received from various sources attractive inducements so to do.

Witness my hand this the 22nd day of January, 1921.

/s/ Jos. B. Long

During the summer of 1921, I had an opportunity to observe the Texas oil operations at first hand and to get acquainted with a different Edgar Cayce. My mother, brother, and I were visiting our grandmother Evans on a small farm outside of Hopkinsville, Kentucky. At fourteen, a farm where I joined a gang with whom I went hunting, swimming, fishing, and experimented with smoking was an adolescent's paradise. But a chance to see an oil well in operation, ride horses, and see cowboys in Texas was like a call to Heaven, at least two steps up from paradise.

I'll never forget our arrival in Comyn, Texas. It had rained. I can't remember it raining any more while I was in Texas, but it had rained there the night before and the mud was a foot deep, cut into black, sticky mush by the wagons and trucks hauling heavy oil well equipment. there was no way to miss it. I stepped off the train into mud that went up over my new white sneakers. I never got them really white again.

The Sam Davis well at Comyn was a mile or so from the town near a Humble Oil tank farm. Farmhouses and shacks surrounded the well. This is where we lived along with the drillers and men who worked on the well. They were about the biggest, toughest, roughest men I'd ever seen. One of the driller's wives, Lenora Ringle, took me under her wing, so to speak, and fed me pie that was almost as good as my grandmother's in Kentucky.

I made friends with several of the younger men, who were only about eighteen or nineteen. The second night I was there, one of them, called "Bud" tapped on my window and asked me if I wanted to go swimming. He was whispering and rather secretive, and I soon found out why. We were going to swim in the small reservoir on the tank farm which supplied the drinking water for the whole area. Dad was talking leases in another cabin, so I joined Bud for a swim. We didn't have bathing suits; he explained that it was better for the water that way. As we walked back, Bud offered me a smoke and launched into some stories that were an education in themselves. I had thought that the members of my gang in Kentucky knew curse words and dirty stories, but Texas oil roustabouts were far, far more explicit and graphic. Dad hadn't come in, so I slipped into bed, but it was a long time before I could go to sleep. I didn't mention the swim to Dad until much later. He didn't seem surprised or comment. The years of Sunday school seemed very far away.

The well itself was fascinating. The heavy drill was lowered by cables from a massive wooden derrick. The drill was linked and short strokes dropped the links one on the other to literally pound a hole into the earth. From time to time, the drill would be pulled up and a slender, hollow instrument they called a bucket lowered to be filled with the shale formation, they called it, through which drilling was progressing. I gathered they had a long way to go, but that everything was proceeding smoothly.

Dad, Dave Kahn, Joe Rush, and a Major Wilson decided to go look at some prospective leases on the Hofstiter ranch near San Antonio. I was told there would be some riding and cowboys. We drove in Joe Rush's Mormon automobile. Dad was on the front seat with Joe and I sat between Dave and the Major on the back seat. It was about the roughest ride I've ever taken. Dave and the Major played a rough game. They pretended their elbows just happened to slip and pound my ribs on either side every time we went over a bump. We didn't see many smooth roads. I fought back but I wasn't any match for either of them, much less the two together. That night when I looked at my ribs, they were blue and turning black. The next day I started yelling so loud they stopped.

Somehow Dad was different from the father and Sunday school

teacher I knew in Selma. He was easy and quiet with the men. They respected him and yet seemed to accept him as one of them. It was as if he had forgotten Selma, yet he didn't raise his voice even when the others argued violently. When we played Texas pitch, called high, low, Jick, Jack, Julie, and game, Dad won repeatedly. Joe Rush was constantly complaining about this and accused Dad of reading his mind. More than once he offered to back him in a gambling venture. Dad kept telling him, smilingly, that the oil well was enough of a gamble for him.

The Hofstiter ranch was everything a fourteen-year-old boy could dream of. We all went riding the day we got there. I was assigned a horse which the foreman explained would be mine while I was on the ranch. We all followed the foreman, and behind us rode one of the cowboys, who had on a curious vest partly formed of matches sewn into the fabric. We passed through field after field of cattle and herds of goats. At one point, the foreman sent me off with the cowboy called Rob to see a ranger shack where he said Zane Grey lived while he wrote *Riders of the Purple Sage*. I could see my cousins back in Kentucky as their eyes popped out when I told them about that cabin. On the way back, Rob explained to me that all I had to do to get the horse to go fast was to let the reins loose on his neck. I did and he took off. Unfortunately, the reins slipped out of my hand as I grabbed for the pommel of the saddle. Rob had to ride alongside and catch the reins or, as he said, "That horse would be running yet."

That night Dad gave a reading and Dave asked him questions about the land over which we had ridden. I can only remember that the reading indicated there wasn't much oil there.

Dad seemed right at home on that ranch. Everyone seemed to like him. He listened to stories and told many I had heard before about his home on the farm, his dog, and the Kentucky Night Riders. I was convinced all over again that my father was the best storyteller I'd ever heard.

When we got back to the well, everyone was upset. A cable had broken and some tools were in the bottom of the hole. "Fishing" for them was a time-consuming, costly process. Dad's reading didn't seem to help very much. Everyone was tense. Some of the men blamed others for the loss of the tools. In trying to keep things quiet, Dave and Dad had to get one of the drillers to put his gun away. The other side had guns, too. I was sure that somebody was about to get shot. Finally they pulled the tools out of the well and everyone celebrated by taking a drink. Some of them acted pretty drunk. Dad then took me into Comyn to get some fried chicken at a little restaurant. The chicken was delicious but I didn't think much of the buttermilk pie.

Dad and Dave decided they had to go east again to raise money. We went by Hopkinsville and Dad stayed a few days, then went on to meet Dave in Atlanta. The search for oil was to go on for another year, to end in failure as the money ran out. Oil traces showed, but leases ran out before wells were drilled to the depth suggested.

CHAPTER 12

Drilled Four Times

In the geographic center of 267,339 square miles of semi-arid land called the State of Texas, in the county of San Saba, Edgar Cayce located what he said would be the largest oil well in Texas. It was drilled four times, twice to the depth he designated. Hundreds of people were directly involved over a period of thirty years. It would be conservative to estimate that at least $200,000 was expended in these operations. At 2000 feet, the gas pressure was strong enough to burn fifteen feet in the air from the hole. None of the wells ever produced oil.

Can we take this as proof of absolute inaccuracy in his readings or is there some possible explanation? Were the wells drilled in the wrong places? With new improved methods could the oil be brought in from the sands, which certainly showed traces? The last man who drilled in this area told me just a short time ago, when I showed him this section, "You give the wrong impressions. You will discredit Edgar Cayce. I'd drill again tomorrow if I had the money. I made the mistakes, not Edgar." You must judge for yourself.

On March 31, 1921, while in New York City at the McAlpin Hotel, Edgar Cayce gave a reading that indicated that drilling had started on February 19, 1921, near San Saba, Texas, and had reached 135 feet by March 14. He said, "This well will produce 40,000 barrels at 2600 feet." From the records this hole was later abandoned far short of the suggested depth because of lack of funds and conflict with the drillers. The Cayce Petroleum Company went broke and lost its leases. Thus ended the first efforts to bring in the "largest oil well in Texas."

W. B. Wyrick, an official of the Western Union Telegraph Company in Chicago, tried to raise funds for a well in San Saba in 1924. On February 15 he wrote to Edgar Cayce, who was then living in Dayton, Ohio, "I am ready to close up the leases in San Saba and start operations as soon as some finances are provided."

It was in this same letter that Wyrick mentioned a geological report on Rocky Pasture in San Saba, for on February 18, 1924, Edgar Cayce wrote Wyrick that Arthur Lammers had the report. This is the same Lammers who asked the questions that initiated the first life reading. On February 25, Edgar Cayce wrote Wyrick that the report was being sent to him. This report was lost. We cannot disregard the possibility that Edgar Cayce's unconscious mind absorbed statements from this report and handed them back in the readings in a rearranged form, though it is certainly unlikely that the report could possibly have contained the details of geologic formations which appeared later in the Cayce psychic readings.

During the time Wyrick was trying to raise money for financing a well, a man we shall call Mr. W. obtained the first of a series of readings on Rocky Pasture in San Saba. Since this first reading may have been the basis for future mistakes, let us examine some of its pertinent details.

The suggestion for the reading given in Dayton on December 29, 1923, was, "In a previous reading [there is no copy in our files] you gave a location west of north of the well that was drilled on J. W. Burns' land as a good place for another well. You will now give specifically the best location south and east of the Burns well for drilling."

In his trancelike state, Cayce answered, "You wouldn't go south and east. Oil strata, yes, but shallow migratory type being that closer to the surface . . . both to north and west and is in the overlap being on the anticline 2900 to 3100 feet."

Question: "Please give the best locations."

Answer: "We have given the best for the locations for it is the best in state or in the continent."

More than two years passed before further information was requested. Then on April 16, 1926, in response to the following suggestion, the second reading was given on Rocky Pasture.

Mrs. C: You will have before you lands in San Saba County, Texas, especially that known as Rocky Pasture, about ten to twelve miles northeast of San Saba, San Saba County, owned by Mrs. Julia A. Moore. You will give the geological lay of Rocky Pasture and vicinity, with reference to the prospects of locating oil. You will make specific location in Rocky Pasture for the drilling of such a well.

Mr. C: (In undertone: They're expecting her to die now.) Yes, we have these lands. We have had these here before [3777 series?] [Mrs. Julia Moor was critically ill.]

Now, in respect to the prospect of oil in this vicinity, and the lay or the geological outlook in this vicinity, we find these conditions exist:

In the Llano uplift, thirty to thirty-five (30 to 35) miles below (South) from this location, we find this land, Rocky Pasture and vicinity, the greater portion of same, is overlaid with the Pennsylvania sand and underlaid with the Two Bend Formations. Little of the cretaceous shows in this vicinity, but to the east there may be seen the outcropping of same, especially on the San Saba Knobs. The formations are such in this vicinity that we find the general lime lays in the angle of north and northwest, and is at near the ninety-four (94) degree, and that there are at least three distinct anticlines that pass through this portion and vicinity of Rocky Pasture. Also, to the south and west there is a cross anticline, forming directly in the farther north that anticline on which Sipe Springs and Erath fields are located.

As to the prospect of oil in this vicinity, we find these conditions then exist, with these *general* outlooks from the surface formation:

There are many sand beds, two to three outcroppings, in Rocky Pasture; of the red beds two to three outcroppings, especially in the Colorado and San Saba Rivers, one lying almost due east or forming the boundary of Rocky Pasture, there is an outcropping of the bend lime. There is also in the San Saba, to the south and west, an outcropping of the bend lime, as is seen, twenty to twenty-two (20 to 22) miles below this the full outcropping of the bend lime, in its natural or original state.

Now we find in the vicinity of Rocky Pasture, lying between this anticline that passes to the east of same, through portion of the adjoining counties, and that on the west in the adjoining counties, where this bend formation and where this cross anticline, on which these northern fields are located, that there is produced in the vicinity of the Rocky Pasture that trap, which may be really called the Mother Pool, or that which has been and is the accumulation of ages, produced by this uplift lying south of this country and vicinity, see? For, as we see, to give the conditions as exist, and as existed in ages past, twice this vicinity has been inundated by the sea. When this uplift was the highest point in this great mountain range, extending all across from the Sierra Cordilleras to that of the White Mountains in New Hampshire. We find this condition was as the backbone, or the ridge, through this whole portion of the continent, and we will find, by drawing a line from that near Monterey in Mexico, on the eastern edge of Cordilleras, to that of near Concord, New Hampshire, that the greater part of the oil fields in the United States are located along the edges, either north or south of this line, as might be drawn. There will also be seen that this edge of San Saba County lies within this range. In the second inundation brought the first and second oil pools and sedimentary conditions to this portion of the uplift, and *under this formation,* which is known as *not* a sedimentary, may the oil be located, in that which may be known as the hickory sands, which will be found to be located in the Rocky Pasture at the *general* depth of twenty-four hundred to three thous d (2400 to 3000) feet from the surface.

In the location then of those for oil in this vicinity, we will find in this a specific manner. There is seen there passes through this tract of land known as Rocky Pasture a gulch, or a gulley, or a creek known as Little and Big Rocky. These join to-gether on the western side of this tract, in the north and western side, about fifty yards from the line of the Murray property, see? In going almost due north from this gulch, thirty paces, we find there a flat or mesa land. That is the place to *drill* for oil, in this portion of Rocky Pasture. There will also be found, near the southwest end, where the outcropping shows a portion of the red bed, and of the enormous lime rock, this would prove a place to drill also. *This* we would find some deeper than that as located near the gulch of Little and Big Rocky Creek, see?

In the drilling we will find and encounter these conditions, for, as we find, there has been drilled, about a thousand and thirty yards, almost east, a little north by east, from this location, a well, to the depth of sixteen hundred (1600) feet. This is at the present time showing indications in the base of this, or where it was drilled to, of the seepage of oil and some gas, as may be seen by the water that may be drawn off from same at the present time.

As to the formations to be encountered, we find then as this:

Through the first eighty (80) feet we will find sand, gravel, sandstone, gravel, lighter shale, and in the loose shale, and just before reaching the sand, at a hundred and twenty to twenty-five (120 to 125) feet, the water will be encountered. This *may* be used for the drilling purpose, or for supplying water for such drilling purposes, for at the one thirty-two to thirty-five (132 to 135) the larger casing may be set, and the water drawn off or used from such. Then we will find we will encounter some black or gray lime, going through this into sand and shale again, until we reach near the depth of nine hundred and sixty-nine feet (969), where we will encounter another heavy lime. There casing should be set again to cut off the water appearing at the three to five hundred (300 to 500) feet level. Then we will encounter the gray lime, with some showing of an oil shale and . . . (steno didn't get the preceding 2 lines) around the one thousand to eleven hundred (1000 to 1100) feet, and through this some two to three hundred (200 to 300) feet, near the fifteen hundred showing (1500), we will encounter some water again. Then, setting casing around the sixteen to seventeen to eighteen hundred (1600 to 1700 to 1800) feet, we will then encounter that sand known as White Mountain, or Cap Mountain, or Green Mountian, and through this encounter the oil shale, and entering the oil bearing sands at near the twenty-six hundred (2600) feet, and we will find a very, very, large production, bringing near to forty, to sixty, to seventy thousand (40,000 to 60,000 to 70,000) *barrels* of crude oil, at a gravity of twenty-nine to forty (29 to 40) in this depth, and the *natural* conditions surrounding this may enable the operators to care for same, see?

We are through. . . . 5628-2.

On May 27, 1926, Edgar Cayce received a letter from Mr. W. indicating that he had brought in three more shallow gas and oil wells, which were producing about fifteen to twenty barrels a day. (These were several counties away.) Mr. W. indicated that he had been to San Saba and was determined to drill by himself. He had, he said, lined up eight thousand acres around the Rocky Pasture location.

Edgar wrote Mr. W. on June 9, 1926, "Hurrah! Hurrah!" He hoped he could go to the well when it was started. In part, Dad wrote in a religious vein, "I am sure you will not fail or falter in keeping your promises to Him. . . . Yet, when we have in heart and purpose broken faith, *then* consternation, fear and trembling enter in, for we, within ourselves, know we haven't kept our promises."

On July 19, 1926, Mr. W. telegraphed, "Tools, supplies and pipe now on rail siding [at San Saba]. Property near your location is in bankruptcy. Am giving them until next Monday or will divert car to Baird, Texas [another county]."

In reply, Dad telegraphed Mr. W. on July 20th, "Location thirty yards north of juncture of Little Rocky and Big Rocky (creeks). As I remember, this is 100 or 50 yards from property line."

Notice that this description was from memory and was not a reading from Edgar Cayce.

Mr. W. wrote to Edgar Cayce on July 29, "No flat mesa land thrity paces north of junction of two said creeks. Old hole is not east of stated location but north and west and is one-half mile from property line instead of 150 yards. Do not go by memory—nothing checks with reports. It is expensive for me. Leases signed."

On rereading the description of the location of the old well from the suggested one for the new well, it seems to me that, using the old well as a "fixed" point of reference, it would have been advisable to measure 1,030 yards west southwest and mark a location, then check it with another reading. It seems wise to question why this was not done when so much was at stake. If one dug on the wrong side of an anticline, the trapped pool could be missed. There is obviously considerable confusion in making the location. One can't help but wonder what property lines are meant.

Dad wrote Mr. W. on the same day he received the above letter. He said that he had a map before him. The location as described was thirty paces north and east from the junction of the Little and Big Rocky Creeks.

A month passed, then Edgar Cayce received a letter from Mr. W. which included the following,

I have gotten together the most complete block in Texas, 17,000 acres all solid and have started the well. I finally got the machine on your exact spot, thirty paces, northeast junction of the two creeks. Sure costs lots to put it there. I was sure disappointed not to get water where you said I would at 125 feet. I am 150 feet deep now and no show of water. Will force me to lay line to water.

He went on to say that an old club-footed local resident was out at the well with an oil man talking about Cayce. Mr. W. said he didn't know Cayce, for he continued: "If it gets out that I am drilling on your location, I can't get any money."

On December 7, Mr. W. wrote that the well was down to 820 feet. He said he hit a hard lime at 776 feet and found a little show of oil. He then closed the well down to go to Oklahoma to sell some leases. When he got back, the hole was full of water. The well was taking more money than he expected, he said. Bills and overdrafts had to be settled by Mr. W. selling his rights in the shallow wells near Baird, Texas. There was no answer from Edgar, and on December 29, Mr. W. wrote again complaining that he hadn't heard from Edgar.

A reading was given on January 1, 1927, which said that shale would be encountered at 1100 to 1200 feet. It was indicated that small production could be taken at 1179 feet, but that large production could be had at 2600 feet. The reading suggested selling Baird interest to put into the San Saba project.

Dad wrote Mr. W. on January 11 of his mother's illness and death, which had caused the delay in getting the reading.

On January 15 Mr. W. wrote that he had to give up the well at 1300 feet. He plugged it and started over 50 feet northeast. He also described the building of a dam on Big Rocky to get water for later use. Thus ended the second drilling effort. It would seem to me that the location was fifty feet further from the original suggestion.

A reading on January 20 indicated that changing locations would affect the depth of some formations which had been described. Production was now predicted for 2689 to be largest in Texas, as much as 50,000 to 75,000 barrels a day. (Note that this is quite a change from the first 30,000 barrels a day.)

A factor must be considered here which may have been known to Edgar Cayce consciously but which did not become a written record until later. Mr. W. drank heavily. Did this affect his judgment on locating the well? Could his attitudes have affected the attunement in terms of the source of the information? For example, the thought patterns of dead oil prospectors would have been very bad sources, especially if they were not recognized. Exaggeration does seem to appear in this reading. A jump from 30,000 to 75,000 barrels is quite a jump.

Mr. W. wrote Edgar Cayce on October 3 that he was telling people he was at 1750 feet but that actually he was at only 1510 feet. He said that so far it had cost him thirty thousand dollars. He was worried about money to finish and wanted to know if the hole had begun to slant at an angle.

Mr. W. wrote encouragingly on December 3, "At 1673 feet I went out of lime. I've gotten more water at 1648. The hole is full of water at 1692. Everyone here tickled. . . . Have bought acreage like wildfire. Cayce, you said it would rain in the last portion of the month and it did on the 30th and 31st. Should I move the boiler back to prevent catching fire?"

A reading of December 13 indicated that money would come in to set the casing. It stated, "A little below the present depth, a heavy lime, drill this near 1823 and set 6⅝ casing. When Penn is again reached (true Penn), we will find the beginning of more than a hundred feet of oil bearing sand. Well to move the boiler."

On February 11, 1928, Mr. W. wrote that he had to run the 6⅝ casing at 1772, the drilling was hard and costing a fortune.

A reading was given on February 17 which suggested the greater change would come at 1823, a sand formation. He described this as "top mountain or hickory or green sand," where there would be the first showing of production. The reading went on to say that there would be white and chalky formations with slate and colored chalk. Again the large pool was mentioned at 2600 feet. Water around the 22nd or 23rd.

Mr. W. said he was down to 1946 on April 15, 1928. He wrote that "the hole is full of water. . . . It filled on the exact day you said it would." He pointed out that the leases were up on October 1, 1928, and wanted to know if he could finish by then.

A reading on April 25 said the depth was 2100 feet. The water, he indicated, should be cut off at 2300 feet and the drilling would not be as hard in the lower part of the strata. Edgar Cayce wrote that he had been ill.

On August 5, Mr. W. wrote that gas and oil were showing. Local people and oil representatives were on hand. One of the men refused to extend the lease so the well was stopped. Mr. W. apparently started a well in another county trying to force the people to extend the leases.

A reading given on August 16 said that the well was at 2487 feet in hard lime. Again, production was promised at 2600 feet.

On September 29, Mr. W. wrote that the leases had been extended for another year and that he had been drilling for two weeks. He said that his other shallow well had been dry. Interest was piling up at $20,000 per year. He was discouraged. Edgar wrote Mr. W. on October 23 that he had been away and sick. He suggested a telegram with questions. A telegram arrived from Mr. W. on December 8, "Am 2576 feet very hard lime. Should I run five-inch pipe now?"

A reading was taken that same day which again indicated oil sand near 2600 feet. It suggested that casing be set so production could be brought in. Warnings of gas and fire were given. A telegram based on this was sent to Mr. W.: "Set casing 2575 feet drill in for success."

In January 1929, Mr. W. tried to reach Dad through my mother's brother in Houston, Texas. The telegram was not delivered and they missed each other.

On January 23, the final reading on the Rocky Pasture, San Saba County, Texas, was given. It still promised success.

This should be drilled to the break in the lime, and then they will reach production that would make the largest producing well in the state and be the largest field in the state. The change in locations make a variation in depths (of information). The present depth is 2674 feet is less than 100 feet of the break in which production would be encountered. Be not discouraged at even striking the hard flint formations—for natural drainages make this the mother pool.

To the end, Edgar Cayce was seemingly certain that production was possible. At that time, such a well would have indeed made a great difference in our father's life story.

Nothing happened. A curtain of silence descended. Mr. W. disappeared. A letter dated March 27, 1935, reached Edgar finally. In part, it read, "Surprised I am at Dr. White's sanitorium. I have been drinking hard since Rocky Pasture was dry." If drinking could solve anything, here was a man, who, in my opinion, had every right to drink. This third effort ended in alcohol.

It is very difficult to tell how deep this well actually was when it was abandoned. From all reports, Mr. W. did considerable drinking prior to entering the sanitorium. Did the movement of the well (as indicated in the reading) make the distance for reaching production greater? Did money and patience run out just short of success? Was the drilling proceeding at an angle as suspected by Mr. W. at one point? Was he confused under the pressures of conflict with lessors, and the need for money? At least one man thought so, for another well was drilled 21 years later using the same set of readings as guidelines.

In September 1950, Mr. R. wrote the following letter to me. (Remember, Dad died in January 1945. This friend had had personal readings while Edgar Cayce was alive, which proved helpful both for physical conditions and accurate on questions dealing with business ventures.)

Dear Hugh Lynn: I went to San Saba, Texas to look for a location described by Edgar Cayce in a reading in 1926. . . . His geology was most unusual and has been borne out by subsequent search except that in thirty years of explorations no *oil* has been found in the county.

I went to the other side of the creek and found Cayce's mesa. I am convinced that Mr. W. drilled in the wrong spot . . . with compass next day, I found he was north six degrees east with his location. My location was north seven degrees west. . . . It was an old Indian camp ground and my sons found arrowheads.

What a wonderful impetus a discovery would give the Association. What great publicity it would be. I will never be satisfied until this site is drilled.

On October 17, 1950, this gentleman wrote to Tom Sugrue, Edgar Cayce's first biographer, "I am leasing some land in San Saba county . . . the geological formation described by Cayce is borne out by all scientific findings. This is an area in which oil will be found in a trap rather than in a widespread formation."

About a week later, I received a letter dated October 24, "I am now working out a deal to drill this well. I made a request for a drilling log and much to my surprise received a drilling log for a well drilled June 19, 1921 by Cayce Petroleum Company of Texas, to a depth of 1626 feet on the same San Saba property." Mr. R. then asked for copies of the readings and went on: "There are dozens of wells in other parts of Texas being bought in every day that would have been considered as dry holes twenty-five years ago."

It was August of 1951 before I received a letter from Mr. R. saying that he had found three wealthy men who could afford to spend $40,000 on the venture. A one-eighth interest was assigned to A.R.E., our research organization, which was preserving and studying the Edgar Cayce data.

Mr. R. began to check Edgar Cayce's descriptions of formations as the new well was drilled. His first report did not arrive until February 4, 1952. It was encouraging.

Your father's geology notified us to expect hard lime at 967 feet. We were to encounter another hard lime before reaching this depth. The first hard lime was encountered and was about 258 feet thick. At 965 feet we encountered a very hard lime which changed to slate at 970 feet. That's right on the button isn't it? The geology also said we would encounter an oil shale between this depth and ten to eleven-hundred feet. We found the oil bearing shale as indicated and the driller reported two rainbows of oil at this depth.

In the same letter, however, two apparent inaccuracies were noted. One was the angle in which the lime was supposed to lie, north and northeast, when in reality it was north and northwest. Mr. R. pointed out that the Gregg shorthand symbols were similar and this may have been a stenographic mistake. He also checked the distance of the two creeks from the Murray property line. It was actually more like 500 yards rather than 50 as given in the reading. From a telegram recorded earlier to Mr. W. when the other well was about to be drilled, Edgar Cayce remembered the distance as about 100 to 150 yards. These details are important in the light of later developments, for they show the thoroughness of Mr. R.'s investigation and his care in checking and following the information in the readings as he understood them.

On February 8, 1952, I wrote to Mr. R. that the stenographer did not use Gregg shorthand and that she said the characters for east and west were quite different. I raised the question of Dad's conscious faulty memory of the surface features, perhaps influencing his descriptions. He had gone over the property and did have a map. The greatest strength of his readings of all kinds lay in the fact that most of them were given at a distance. I also asked if Murray had at any time owned land closer to the two creeks. Mr. R. checked this. Murray had never owned any other property in the area.

On the 18th of February, Mr. R. reported trouble with a crevice in the hard lime. The drill at 1485 feet was going off at an angle. The hole was filled with rocks and metal and drilling continued. On the 25th of February, Mr. R. wrote that water was encountered at 1500 feet just as indicated in the reading.

During the following month, I visited the well and can remember being impressed by the samples of various formations through which the drilling had progressed. They checked accurately, according to Mr. R., with the readings.

Mr. R. reported on April 4, 1952, that a pin had been sheared off of the 1500-pound drill and that it was 2000 feet down in the hole. They grappled for it for two weeks.

On May 9, Mr. R. reported to one of the A.R.E. trustees that 70 quarts of nitroglycerin were set off in the hole and that gas flared to ten feet in the air.

Mr. R. wrote on June 7 that a nice show of oil appeared at 2487 feet, just where the readings said it would be. Then, in a telegram on June 25, he indicated that they were drilling in cap lime and had encountered oil shale at 2750 feet. A few days later Mr. R. reported that he had leased 6500 additional acres. He also brought in a heavy control head to handle the pressure. Excitement ran high and then cooled off as another bit was lost in the hole, involving a delay of six weeks.

Drilling was finally begun again in very hard formation. They were making only two feet a day. By October 7, 1952, the hole was down to 3206 feet. The driller's contract was for 3000 feet so he demanded more money. Finally, by December 31, 1952, Mr. R. reported that the hole was abandoned at 3520 feet. The fourth and final drilling effort was over.

Suddenly the excitement ended. The possibility of having finances from oil to carry out research based on the readings was over. Again questions have to be faced. This time greater care was taken in locating the well. Greater depth was reached. In fact, this last well was drilled to more than 1000 feet below the production depth described in Edgar Cayce's first readings on this area and confirmed many times in subsequent readings. Oil can't run away without leaving traces of its passing. Was the location correct? Could the first well drilled by Mr. W. have been nearer correct? Could the first well drilled by Mr. W. have been nearer correct? Did Mr. R. simply miss the deep pool? Would a fifth attempt be successful?

Today Mr. R. says,

We did not drill the well as an oil man would have drilled it. I hunted up the man who had worked for Mr. W. He repeated his mistakes. We should have drilled with a rotary drill with a new man with the old driller as consultant.

Today water can be controlled. When we drilled that well eighteen years ago very little was known about controlling water pressure in comparison with today's techniques."

Consider another possibility. If Edgar Cayce's information was incorrect, what made it so? Did his unconscious simply fabricate and piece the readings together from the geological report, his talks with oil men, and his visit to Rocky Pasture in San Saba? So many times he seems to have been partly right, especially for others. Is this just a "made-up" ego justification? Or could Edgar Cayce, hoping for money for his hospital which was under pressure, have taken information from sources which were inaccurate, such as the minds of hopeful oil prospectors living and dead? Is it possible that the ideal we hold in seeking psychic information from self or others controls the attunement and thus designates the source from which information can be secured? Such examples as set forth here certainly give any investigator a reason for concern and suggest that standards and purposes must be clearly defined. We insist again that these apparent failures may be able to tell us as much or more about psychic perception as the thousands of accurate successes.

Of course, there is one more reason or explanation of why some of the readings may seem inaccurate. Maybe it was simply that no one truly followed the directions and looked in the right place. Some readings on buried treasure were never checked out or were explored poorly. At first thought, this seems incredible. But when one rereads the information, the reasons become apparent. The location may have been so remote or difficult to get to that considerable time, effort, and money had to be expended to conduct even a perfunctory search. The person requesting the reading may have been too poor, too uneducated, or too unskilled to conduct a thoroughly scientific expedition. The information given in the reading may have been so vague and indefinite that it was impossible to pinpoint a precise location to excavate. Good metal detectors were not available then (most of the treasure readings were given in the early twenties and thirties, before the development of modern metal locators). In most cases, so much time has elapsed since the original readings that the landmarks referred to have been obliterated.

Unfortunately, some or all of the above conditions apply in every reading on lost mines, oil wells, or buried treasure. These factors are not offered as a full explanation for Edgar Cayce's failure to produce a chest of Spanish doubloons. However, these points should furnish a setting not only for judging any Cayce reading, but for considering psychic data from any source. Consider the possible sources. Consider the factors likely to direct a psychic to a particular source. Finally consider the record of the particular psychic.

In the case of Edgar Cayce, there are probably less than 200 readings out of 14,246 of the type we have considered in this book. If Cayce were completely wrong in every one of these, his accuracy could still be over 98%. In fact, his accuracy has been estimated by medical researchers to be in the neighborhood of 85% to 90%.

CHAPTER 13

Indian Gold in Arkansas

Let's look at one case that you might think should have been found, because this reading was given voluntarily without any prior suggestion. At the end of the reading were the instructions, "Give this to Jones." The "Jones" referred to was not related to the person for whom the first reading was given. Seldom did Edgar Cayce give a reading without a specific request or suggestion. In the rare cases that he did, there was usually a strong desire on the part of the person or some pressing reason for him giving the reading. For example, a woman had been thinking of writing Edgar Cayce for a physical reading. Finally she wrote to him at Virginia Beach. However, Cayce was in New York at the time and did not receive the letter because it was not forwarded to him. At the end of a reading he had given in New York, without any suggestion, he gave a reading for this woman whose letter he had not received. He suggested emergency treatments, which were airmailed to the woman. It was only when he returned to Virginia Beach later that he discovered the woman had actually written for a reading.

Why he should have given this reading for a Mr. Jones in Texas about a buried treasure in Arkansas is not known. From the information given, it sounds as if some dead relatives of Mr. Jones were anxious for him to find the buried money. Maybe Cayce picked up this desire and transmitted the information. For whatever reason, here is the story.

Without any suggestion or request, Edgar Cayce began the following reading immediately after another one concerning an oil well in Texas. The time was 4:00 P.M. on April 27, 1925.

Now, we are locating these conditions as surround the monies and the bullion as was buried by the Indians here in the Southeastern part of Washington, County, Arkansas, near Boston Mountain. Inquiry made by Indian and a relative of those that cached same.

The camp as made or occupied here, 60 odd—63, 65, 67 years ago, near Boston line mountain, (the camp) and the maps as were made by Soohoo buried these with—Cordi—one to the East, one to the West, while the Spring is to the West of old camp site. A line running East and West from map to map we find would come through portion of camp, and were a line made from West spot of the map and from the East map we would find same would cross just North of the Spring and on edge of a ravine, which slopes run East and West. This we find on upper slope, South side, yet North slope. Some thirty (30) steps from Spring the cache, which is near now a clump of Hazelnut bushes and a long (Chestnut log) comes across the edge. The cache is in triangle rock, covered by another, and is only twenty-seven (27) inches deep. We will find all nearly the amount when coined of two hundred thousand (200,000) dollars, gold silver.

Give this to "Jones."

We are through. . . . 3982-1

When this reading was forwarded to Mr. Jones, he was naturally quite excited. He wrote back that he had told his father of the reading and his father was as excited as he was. His father knew where the old Indian camp was, "on a high flat mountain about 14 miles west of Winslow on the old Jimmie York Place." Furthermore, long ago, his father had found one map about a mile and a half east of the campground and destroyed it. The other map about 300 yards west of the camp was not destroyed. Mr. Jones requested additional information because, since one map was gone, it would not be possible to project a line between the maps. He enclosed a sketch with his letter. Unfortunately, the sketch was not to scale and was so poorly drawn that it was scarcely decipherable.

Edgar Cayce wrote back asking for a little better sketch so that directions given from it would be understandable. This sketch, too, while better than the first, was roughly drawn and had no scale. Mr. Jones wrote, "I will try to make the drawing plainer but old dad can't read or write and I just have to draw it the way he tells me. Also, he hasn't been there for several years." He also wrote than an Indian nephew had hunted for the money near one of the maps but he didn't think he was searching near the right one. The map that remained was drawn on a big flat rock. Jones and his father and a brother planned to go look for this treasure in July, which was as soon as all of them could get a vacation. Meanwhile, they were eagerly awaiting any additional information Edgar Cayce could or would give. They requested that Edgar Cayce come to Arkansas and go treasure-hunting with them if he could. However, they warned that it might be best to let them go and get acquainted first because the property owners were "moonshiners and outlaws" and wouldn't let a stranger stop near there.

On June 5, before Mr. Jones left Texas for Arkansas, he wrote to Edgar Cayce again. The fever of his excitement had had time to cool and he was having some misgivings.

Have asked for our vacations the first of July and guess we will get it then if something doesn't happen. Dad has been telling me the Indians put a bad wish on that money when they buried it and he was afraid the evil spirits would try to keep us away from it. Do you think there is such a thing as that? If anything like that should happen what would be the thing to do?

The letter continued with questions of how to handle the money if it were found.

Edgar Cayce wrote back:

June 11, 1925

Dear Mr. Jones:

I have yours of the 5th. I note what you have to say regarding the superstition of the Indians. I have heard some people tell of such conditions. I personally do not feel that there is anything in this kind of superstition, though I myself have never had any experience with anything of the kind, but am of the opinion you have need of no fear regarding anything pertaining to that, and would feel like that you would rather have the assistance of such than their hindrance, should there be anything in such, else why would they have given the location of same and desire that it be used for the purposes, for if there be one perhaps there are other phases of this same superstition and unless they had desired that you seek this out and put it to use, the information as given would not have been gotten, and if you will notice the reading of same, which I'm sure you must have, there is particular mention made that the desires are that this be sought out and put to use. I'm sure the best plan would be to carry this to some bank and deposit same until the division is made.

With kindest personal regards.
Edgar Cayce

Mr. Jones wrote again on June 30, 1925, that they were preparing to leave for Arkansas. They planned to drive a stake somewhere on the old Indian campground and then request another reading in which directions were to be given from the stake.

On July 6, 1925, edgar Cayce received the following telegram:

WINSLOW ARK 6 1030A
EDGAR CAYCE
322 GRAFTON AVE DAYTON OHIO
STAKE HAS BEEN DRIVEN WIRE INSTRUCTIONS AT ONCE

That afternoon Edgar Cayce gave the following reading:

Mrs. C: You will have before you lands in Washington County, Arkansas, near Boston Mountain, and the treasure buried there, information regarding same that you gave in a reading on April 27, 1925, and a stake on these lands, placed there by Jones, to whom you said this information should be given. Please locate this treasure in reference to the stake as placed by Jones in a definite and concise manner, giving in literal words the message that should be sent to Jones at this time.

Mr. C: Yes, we have the treasure here as placed there some seventy odd years ago, with information as given on April 27th regarding same. Now, we find the stake as placed is near the spring that has cropped out or begun since placing of treasure, and that the opening or spring which now shows is only a decavity or a low place, with rock (cope shape) above same. The stake as driven is thirty and one-tenth (30 and 1/10) yards to the South and East of the treasure. This near where a log lies across a rock. Now below this rock we find a small dogwood tree, with a vine growing on same. This vine, however, not a clinging vine, rather bramble briar like; between this rock and the dogwood, we would find the treasure. Two hundred thousand dollars bullion, with other precious stones.

This wire then:

North and West from stake to side of hill where dogwood below projecting rock. Between rock and dogwood lies treasure. Dig there. Full information in mail at this address. . . .3892–2

Surely this information was specific. It sounds as if one should be able to find the exact spot easily from a driven stake; but on July 9, 1925, the following wire arrived: RECEIVED LETTER SECOND STAKE DRIVEN WIRE INSTRUCTIONS.

Edgar Cayce promptly gave another reading:

Mrs. C: You will have before you lands in Washington County, Arkansas, near Boston Mountain, and the treasure buried there, information regarding same that you gave in a reading on April 27, 1925, and the second stake on these lands, placed there by Jones, to whom you said this information should be given. Please locate this treasure in reference to the stake as placed by Jones, in a definite and concise manner, giving in literal words the message that should be sent at this time.

Mr. C: Yes, we have the information and the treasure here. In reference to this second stake, we find the location of same is just the length of the height of Jones from stake, South by East from stake, North by West from treasure to stake. Then this wire:

The length of self from stake, South by East, location.

Q–1. Is the location nearer the South point than the East point, or about half way?

A–1. Just as given. South by East, length of body of Jones. We find there are marks on the ledge above where this is located, pointing in opposite direction from same. Then taking stake in the earth, the direction as pointed would be opposite from that as is indicated on the rock. South by East, see? Five feet, nine and a quarter (5 ft. 9¼ ") inches.

Q-2. Any other information for Jones at this time?

A-2. This is what was asked for. This is given. . . . 3982-3

How can you get closer than this? Less than six feet south by east from this second stake lay $200,000. Too bad these treasure-hunters didn't have a modern metal detector. It would have saved much useless digging.

Edgar Cayce was concerned, too, about this treasure hunt, and wrote the treasure-hunters a personal letter.

Your wire received this morning and this was taken at once, and the wire sent you as follows:

"Length of self from stake South by East location. See letter."

I certainly hope that you have no trouble in making the location and I feel sure you will make it without any trouble. It may be a little earth over the first rock, then you will find the rock over the treasure itself buried between a triangle rock.

Let me hear from you. You know if I can be of help I want to.

Sincerely,
Edgar Cayce

Evidently there was a phone call from Mr. Jones as there is no letter or wire requesting this fourth reading. The treasure hunters must have spent some time digging futilely.

Mrs. C: You will have before you the lands in Washington County, Arkansas, near Boston Mountain, and the treasure as has been located there is a reading. They have reported that they found location as given, in last reading, without success. You will please tell us what is the fault with this and if this is not the proper location where may this be found. Please dictate wire to be sent to Jones at this time.

Mr. C: Send this wire: The location where digging in opposite direction from that given from stake.

Now, we have these conditions as regarding this treasure. Make these locations specific from these lines. We find this treasure was buried by Indian who came from camp that was to the East of this location. There are, as we see, many springs (now four in number). At the time five in number, when burial was made. A line drawn from camp to the two markers as the directions show in the maps that were left, the one to the East, the one to the West. These, as we see, where this should be is toward the West from the camp site. The springs to the South and the Spring to the South and East, the Springs to the South and East now running. The location then was made from that one now existent. The one now not showing, with the coping shape rock above same, where the location of the present buried treasure. This may be found. Seek and ye shall find, for this is given as the benefit to those to whom this is payable.

Q-1. Did they make the location just opposite from the stake as was given in last reading?

A-1. Just given. Send then this wire: Location made opposite direction as given from stake. Sign. . . . 3982-4

This information was forwarded to Mr. Jones as was the following reading, which again was spontaneous and unsolicited. It was given on July 11, 1925, right after another reading, for someone not related to the treasure-hunters.

Mr. C: Now, we have the prospecting location here, as Mr. Jones is seeking for, near Boston Mountain, in the Southeastern portion of Washington County, Arkansas. The location as has been staked out at present is in the area of the treasure, and with spreading out of same a little to the South and East, he should be able to locate same.

Q-1. How much should he spread out?

A-1. Two feet.

Q-2. Anything further regarding this?

A-2. This information may be useful, unless they spread farther as they work in this. . . . 3982 5

On August 1, 1925, Edgar Cayce received a letter from Mr. Jones from Texas saying that the treasure-hunting party had returned home empty-handed. He reported:

Dear Mr. Cayce,

I have been trying to get a chance to write you ever since we came back. We left there July 15. Sure hated to give it up but we done all we could, and I am sure you did, but there was some mistake somehow. I carried a compass so we would make no mistake in the direction. We found the spring and drove first stake that put us on a ridge, but the second stake put us on slope of the ravine, it had about 15 yards slope from top to bottom of the ravine. The second stake was about 5 yards from the bottom and a long dead log lay about four feet to the south of the second stake, but there was no rocks. We dug the hillside off nearly and every place you told us but could not find the rocks. We then worked like the indian told dad and looked for two surface rocks east of the map. We did find several and dug in them all but never did find anything.

This letter continues with some other nonpertinent information and closes with hope that he can go back some day and continue the search.

What went wrong here? Originally there seems to be no reason to question motives since the first information regarding this treasure was unsolicited. The question of where the information came from may be important, and the time element may be involved, when was Edgar Cayce describing the location of this cache? at the time it was buried or in 1925? Was there any confusion about the stakes or the compass directions taken by Mr. Jones from the stakes? How many degrees did Edgar Cayce mean when he said south by east? Was this from true north or magnetic north? Mr. Jones said he used only a crude compass, not a transit. An error of even 3 degrees would make a difference of approximately 6 feet in 100 feet.

Nothing was said about how big a hole was dug or how deep. He could have missed it by a foot or so. Without mechanical equipment there is a limit to the amount of dirt that can be moved in two or three days by one or two men. I doubt if Mr. Jones's father did much digging since he is referred to as an old man. Also, they reported that when they found no rock on the surface near the dogwood they began digging under nearby surface rocks. It sounds like they did a lot of useless digging under nearby rocks instead of digging exactly where the reading suggested.

It is certainly unfortunate that the search party did not have a modern metal detector. Unless the cache for some reason (landslides, floods, or other earth movements) has gotten much deeper, it should be easy to locate with a modern metal detector or metal locator. If I were going treasure-hunting this location would probably be my choice to start with especially since there is no extraneous metal (such as exists at Kelly's Ford in the form of battle debris) to confuse the locator. Also, the depth is not excessive as in the case of White Hill. Of course, these readings were given 43 years ago. Has the land changed much? Could one still locate the old campground, the springs, the map on the rock? Has the treasure been dug up in these intervening years?

I don't know, but it might be worth a try. Anyone for $200,000?

CHAPTER 14

The Outer Limits

We are so used to dealing with our everyday physical world that we forget our sense limitations. We tend to classify all our experiences within a framework of "normal" perception. What is "normal" perception? Is it normal to look through a telescope and see craters on the moon, rings around Saturn, or the faint luminosity of a distant galaxy? Is it normal to peer into a microscope and realize that another world, complete with living creatures whose being we never dreamed of, exists in a drop of water?

Dogs hear sounds beyond the range of our ears. There are insects whose sense of smell makes our nose a very coarse instrument indeed. Our sight includes only a tiny fraction of the electromagnetic spectrum. With infra-red cameras, radio, radar and television we are able to probe further into this endless radiation. Is there a whole new world, or a different way of looking at the one we know, just beyond the range of our five senses? Can we learn to extend the range of these senses, or develop new ones?

Through the psychic perception of our father, Edgar Cayce, we, along with thousands of persons who have examined his reports, have come to consider the existence of this "world we never knew before." Is it so strange to find now and then an individual whose perception extends beyond what we consider normal? When we do find such a person, must we write him off as a charlatan if his every report from his strange new world is not 100 percent verifiable? Do we not forget that our own vision is limited in foggy weather, and we are sometimes fooled by optical illusions? Our own ears cannot hear a bird's song over the roar of a jet plane. Our marvelous electrical creations, radio and television sets, are sometimes jammed with unaccountable static and we do not always enjoy perfect reception. Is there not a similarity here? Selfishness, ego, negative thought patterns, littleness of purpose, wrong suggestions, bad settings, are the static which seem to block and distort psychic perception.

Now and then there were reports which seemed to touch a universal stream of mind-spirit. It is this stretching to the outer limits which creates the real challenge to the man who would bind himself to matter, but it also inspires the seeker, all seekers, to strive for greater attunement with the Creative Mind, the Universal Consciousness which many call God.

What we have tried to do in this book is analyze the apparent failures of a remarkable psychic, Edgar Cayce, in an attempt to learn more about the nature and limits of such abilities. Hopefully, this glimpse of the outer limits of psychic perception will sharpen our wits for the journey beyond.

P A R A V I E W

PARAVIEW
publishes quality works that focus on body, mind,
and spirit; the frontiers of science and culture;
and responsible business—areas related to
the transformation of society.

PARAVIEW PUBLISHING
offers books via four imprints.

PARAVIEW POCKET BOOKS
are traditionally published books co-published by Paraview
and Simon & Schuster's Pocket Books.

PARAVIEW PRESS, *PARAVIEW SPECIAL EDITIONS,* and
PARAVIEW CLASSICS use digital print-on-demand
technology to create original paperbacks for niche audiences,
as well as reprints of previously out-of-print titles.

For a complete list of **PARAVIEW** Publishing's books
and ordering information, please visit our website at
www.paraview.com, where you can also sign up
for our free monthly media guide.

TRANSFORMING THE WORLD
ONE BOOK AT A TIME

Printed in the United States
52341LVS00002B/577-657